A Garland Series

The English Stage
Attack and Defense 1577 - 1730

A collection of 90 important works
reprinted in photo-facsimile in 50 volumes

edited by
Arthur Freeman
Boston University

A Second Defence of
the Short View of
the Prophaneness and Immorality
of the English Stage

by

Jeremy Collier

with a preface
for the Garland Edition by

Arthur Freeman

Garland Publishing, Inc., New York & London

1972

Library of Congress Cataloging in Publication Data

Collier, Jeremy, 1650-1726.
  A second defence of the Short view of the prophaneness
[sic] and immorality of the English stage.

   (The English stage: attack and defense, 1577-1730)
   Reprint of the 1700 ed.
   "Wing C5262."
   1. Drake, James, 1667-1707. The antient and modern
stages survey'd. 2. Theater--Moral and religious
aspects. 3. Theater--England. I. Title. II. Series.
PN2047.C62D72 1972   792'.013   76-170445
ISBN 0-8240-0617-8

Printed in the United States of America

Preface

Chronologically, Jeremy Collier's Second Defence *of his 1698* Short View *follows the reflections on his original* Defence *by James Drake and John Oldmixon, though it is entirely addressed to confuting the former.* Drake's Antient and Modern Stages Survey'd *was advertised as published "this day" by* The Post Boy, *March 11-14, and in the same periodical nearly a year later (8-10 February 1700) the* Second Defence *is recorded, again as "This Day is Publish'd"; but Collier's short preface (perhaps on an inserted leaf) dates it 26 November 1699. At any rate a substantial time had elapsed, given the rapid earlier cut-and-thrust replies, due to what Collier claims was his engagement "in Business for the Press" (presumably volumes one and two of* The Great Historical, Geographical, Genealogical, and Poetical Dictionary*), and his doubts of the wisdom of replying at all — "had it not been for the Charge of false Quotation." By now, surely, the controversy was aging into staleness, and not until Edward Filmer's* Defence of Plays *did any*

5

PREFACE

serious re-engagement transpire. Collier's future antitheatrical writings (1703, ?1704, 1708) are mere squibs by comparison, the arena now being left to the scholastic likes of Bedford and Law.

Our reprint is prepared from a copy of the original edition in the possession of the Publishers, collating $\pi^1 A^1 B\text{-}I^8 K^7$, compared with British Museum copies 641.e.8 and Ashley 445. A1, "To the Reader," is likelier the "extra" or inserted leaf, $\pi 1$ being imposed with K^7.

Lowe-Arnott-Robinson 293; Hooker 27; Wing C 5262; Ashley X, 81.

July, 1972   A. F.

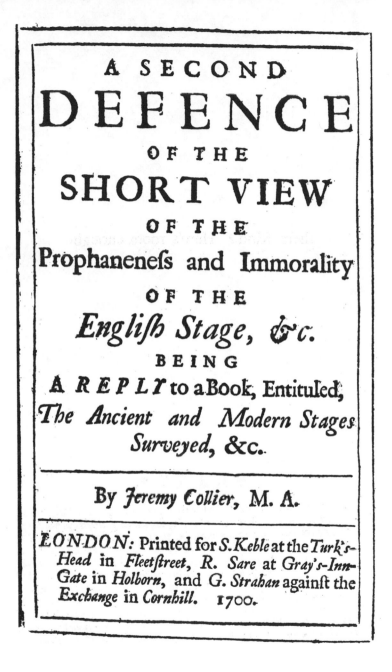

A SECOND DEFENCE

OF THE

SHORT VIEW

OF THE

Prophaneneſs and Immorality

OF THE

Engliſh Stage, &c.

BEING

A *REPLY* to a Book, Entituled,

The Ancient and Modern Stages Surveyed, &c.

By *Jeremy Collier*, M. A.

LONDON: Printed for *S. Keble* at the *Turk's-Head* in *Fleetſtreet*, *R. Sare* at *Gray's-Inn-Gate* in *Holborn*, and *G. Strahan* againſt the *Exchange* in *Cornhill*. 1700.

ERRATA.

PAge 20. line 5. for *of them* read *of the Poem*, p. 21. Margin, for *ssset* r. *esses*, p. 28. l. 30. Margin, for *nempit* r. *erupit*. p. 29. l. 19. Margin, for *immodestiæ* r. *immodestia*, p. 50. l. 18. for *discourr'd* r. *discours'd*, p. 51. l. 24. for , r.: p. 53. l. 13. for *Epithe* r. *Epithet*, p. 71. l. 5. for *this* r. *his*, p. 72. l. 24. for *Poet* r. *Poet's*, Ibid. l. 30. for *Prometheus* r. *Prometheus*, p. 73. l. 1. for *Prometheus* r. *Prometheus*, Ibid. for Αναϛίας r. Αναϛίας, p. 78. l. 33. for *Under Character* r. *Under Characters*, p. 88. l. 3. for *Sx* r. *Six*, p. 97. l. 33. dele *as I remember*, p. 101. l. 23. for *Selecism* r. *Solecisme*, p. 105. l. 29. for *Charges* r. *Charge*, p. 120. l. 5. for *Dramatists* r. *Dramàtist*, p. 127. l. 5. for *Law* r. *Laws*, p. 128. l. 19. for *belongs* r. *belong*, p. 134. l. 16. for τροϡμ r. πραϡει.

To the Reader.

WHen my Adversary first appear'd, I was engaged in Business for the Press, which I could not well dismiss, till 'twas brought somewhat forward. Besides, I was sometime at a stand whether to Answer, or not, and, I think, had left my Book to take its Fate, had it not been for the Charge of false Quotation.

As to the Author of the Survey, &c. his Manner is all over extraordinary, but in what relates to my Authorities, I think altogether unpresidented; such a size of Assurance, so unsupported by Proof and Colour, is rarely to be met with. If he continues to cast the Cause thus entirely upon his Courage, he must Dispute by himself.

His Eagerness to Defend the Stage, has sometimes transported him into plain Rudeness: To this I shall only observe, That Railing is a scandalous Talent, and an Argument of an ill Undertaking. When a Man throws Dirt, 'tis a sign he has no other Weapon. These are Unchristian

A   *and*

and *Ungentlemanly Sallies*, *and not so much as* allow'd *to Provocation.* Having *therefore neither Liberty, nor Fancy for this way,* I *shall, for the most part, over-look his Misbehaviour.*

As for the Stage, I *almost despair of doing them any Service:* They *are more enclin'd,* I *perceive, to Repeat their Faults then amend them:* They *make no scruple of coming over again with their* Ill Plays; As *if Immodesty and Prophaneness were the more valuable for being discover'd.* But *thus to bear up against Evidence, and go on in Defiance of Religion, is an odd Instance of Resolution. And besides the ill Colour of the Quality, 'twill fail us at the long Run:* Courage without Conscience *starts at the other World, and leaves a Man dispirited when he has most need of Support.* To Consider that *we have done our Utmost to Debauch Mankind, will be no Pleasure at such a Juncture as This. Unless therefore we could Demonstrate the Grounds of Atheism, Common Sense, if minded, will put us upon a Provision beyond the Grave.*

Novemb. 26. 1699.   AN

AN
ANSWER

To a BOOK, Entituled,

The Ancient and Modern Stages Surveyed, &c.

BEfore I proceed farther with my Adverſary, it may not be amiſs to obſerve, that his Scheme is defective, and the Compaſs of his Defence much ſhort of the Charge. For he does not apply his Anſwer to any Particulars, nor ſo much as Vindicate one Paſſage accuſed of Indecency and Irreligion. So that were his whole Book true, the Imputation of *Prophaneneſs* and *Immorality,* would ſtill lie heavy upon the *Stage.* This Author, to give him ſome part of his Character, ſeems to rely more upon Stratagem and Surprize, than plain Force, and open Attack. His Buſineſs is all along to perplex the Cauſe and amuſe the *Reader,* and to Reaſon, and Repreſent amiſs. In the firſt place he tells us a Story,

which

The *Ancient and Modern Stages Sur-veyed*, &c. P. 7, 8 9. P. 13, 23.

which Mr. *Rymer* had told before, about the Original of *Plays* ; and charges all the *Immorality*, and Diforders of the *Stage*, upon the Head of Idolatry, and the Practice of the *Mimes* and *Pantomimes*. And when he has thus entangled the Difpute, and like the Scuttle-Fifh mudded the Water, he thinks himfelf out of Reach ; but I fhall endeavour to dive after him, and drag him to the furface.

In his Hiftory of Heathenifm and the Stage, he lays down feveral unlucky Affer-tions, and ruines himfelf in his very De-fence. He lets us know, that *Paganifm*

The *Ancient and Modern Stages Sur-veyed*, &c. p. 10.

was invented to oblige and captivate the People, and gain'd its Authority among them by in-dulging their Senfuality, and gratifying their Lufts : That the Games and Shewes were the moft engaging parts of their Religion, and that

P. 12, 13.

the Devotional and Pompous part of their Worfhip, was ungrateful to the Spectators, who impatiently expected the Shew. He informs us farther, That the Fathers thought it not fafe *to truft their Converts to the Temptations of fo jolly a Religion, that the Portion of thofe that embraced Chriftianity was Mortifi-cation, that their Reward was in Reverfion, and that prefent Enjoyment is apt to prevail againft a remote Hope.*

Now if Stage-Plays were fuch Licen-tious Diverfions, if they indulged Sen-fuality and Luft, feifed fo powerfully upon People's Inclinations, and made them for-

forget the Interests of *Futurity* ; If the Case stood thus, (as the *Surveyor* confesses) then there were other heavy Articles against the *Stage* besides *Idolatry* ; Then the bold Liberties and Luscious Pleasures of the Place, were sufficient Reasons why the Fathers declaimed against it ; and by consequence their Censures come strong upon the *English* Theatre.

The Infancy of Christianity and the frequency P. 14, 15. *of Persecutions,* don't alter the Measures of Behaviour, nor make so great a difference between the Primitive and Modern Christians, as our Author would suppose. If 'tis possible, we have more Reason to be cautious and self-denying, than those who lived in the first Ages of our Religion. For then the History of our *Faith* was fresh, and the Proofs lay nearer to the *sense*. Then Miracles were frequent to refresh their Memory, and quicken their Zeal. Besides their very Sufferings were awakening Circumstances, and a Guard upon their Virtue. Their being so ill used in this World, was naturally apt to make them take the more care about the other. Having none of these Advantages, we have more need of Discipline and Recollection ; and should stand as much aloof from Temptation as ever. And therefore whatever debauches our Appetites, overheats our Affections, and, as our Author Phrases it, *relaxes the Nerves of our Zeal,* P. 38.

ought

ought by all Means to be avoided.

The *Surveyor* is now going to take off the Censure of the Fathers from the Stage. And here he begins with St. *Augustine*, who (says he) *absolves their Comedies and Tragedies from any fault in the Expression, and accuses only the subject Matter.*

P. 22.

To this I Answer ;

First, That St. *Augustine*'s Charge against the Play-houses runs very high ; he look'd upon them as no better than the Nurseries of Lewdness and Irreligion, and comprehended Comedy amongst the rest of their Performances ; as appears by his Instance in *Roscius* ; but these Testimonies were too troublesome for the *Surveyor* to take notice of.

View, &c. p. 273, 274, 275.
Defence, &c. p. 85, 86.

Secondly, St. *Augustine*, even in this place, blames Comedies and Tragedies for being very foul and faulty in their *Fable* and Matter, * and by consequence could not think them proper for Christian Diversion.

* *Multa rerum turpitudine.*

Thirdly, St. *Augustine* does not say that Comedies, *&c.* were always clean in the Expression. He throws in a Sentence which qualifies the Proposition, and makes it affirm no farther, than that they were not so smutty as *many other things.* 'Tis probable he might mean they were not so rank as the *Bacchanal* and *Floral* Solennities.

Nulla, saltem sicut alia multa, verborum obscenitate composita. De Civit. Dei Lib. 2. Cap. 8.

But

But thefe Words, *Sicut alia multa*, which change the Sence, and make clearly againſt him, he is pleaſed to omit in the *Engliſh*, tho they ſtand ſtaring in the Margin, and are part of his own Quotation. To fal-ſifie thus in the face of Conviction, is like Stealing before the *Bench :* But thus he is pleaſed to detect himſelf, and to give us a noble Diſcovery of his Honeſty and Cun-ning, at his firſt ſetting out. However he would do well not to rely too much upon an *Engliſh* Reader for the future.

This Gentleman advances to the Teſtimo-nies cited by the *View, &c.* And here he is pleaſed to skip quite over the Councils, and takes no notice of above half the Fathers, and thoſe he has the Courage to undertake, he does but touch at. And thus he con-futes a Book at the rate that Mice do, only by nibbling a little at a few of the Leaves. However I muſt attend him in his Method. Let us therefore conſider that little he can afford us from *Clemens Alex-andrinus* ; where this Father affirms, That *the Circus and Theatre may not improperly be called the Chair of Peſtilence.* Here the Sur-veyor would know, *whence it appears that the Dramatick Exerciſes are here aimed at ?* Were the *Mimi* and *Pantomimi* leſs *con-cerned with the Stage ?* &c.   P. 24.

In anſwer to theſe Queſtions the Reader may pleaſe to underſtand, that the Sur-veyor makes great uſe of the Diſtinction

be-

between the *Drama* (as he calls it) and
the *Mimi* ; by this means he hopes to perplex the Controverfy, and divert the Cenfure of the Fathers, as if in their Opinion
Comedy and Tragedy were inoffenfive Diverfions ; but I fhall endeavour to make
this Evafion unferviceable to him, by
fhewing,

Firft, That feveral of the Fathers, as appears by the *View, &c.* cenfure Tragedy and
Comedy by name. Nay, thus much the
Surveyor himfelf confeffes, that *Tragedy and
Comedy is fometimes condemned for Company.*
Now if *Comedy* is jointly condemned with
the *other Shews* of the *Theatre*, why does
he endeavour to make the Fathers juftifie
or overlook it ? Why fo much pains to
take off their Cenfure, and point the Satyr
another way ? What needs all this rattling
with *Mimes, Pantomimes,* and *Drama*, as if
there was fome Charm and Myftick Power
in the Words ? If the Fathers condemn
Comedy, *&c.* exprefly, 'tis to no purpofe
to conteft their Sence, and pretend their
Opinion undeclared. He muft own therefore the *Ancients* are full againft him in
the Point. And fince Comedy and Tragedy is thus exprefly condemned by the *Fathers*, we have reafon to believe it always
comprehended under their general Cenfure
of the *Stage.* Which will appear farther
if we confider

Ibid. (margin)

Secondly,

Secondly, That Comedy and Tragedy were the principal and moſt frequent Diverſions on the Stage.

That they were the principal, I ſuppoſe the *Surveyor* will allow, upon the account of the *Fable*, and the Advantage of the Plot and *Characters :* The *Mimi* being form'd upon little Subjects, and Vulgar Perſons *. [*] *Lilius Gyraldus de Poet. Hiſt. Dial. 6.*

That *Comedy, &c.* were the moſt frequent Diverſions of the Stage, I prove thus ;

Firſt, Becauſe the *Mimi*, Dancing on the Stage, *&c.* were Originally part of Comedy, as we may learn from *Suetonius* ; and ſo in all likelihood they continued a great while. *Diomedes libr. 3. in Fragm. Sueton. primis temporibus ut aſſerit Tranquillus, Omnia quæ in ſcena verſentur in Comœdia agebantur ;*

Secondly, The Poets who wrote the *Mimi* or *Farces* were very few, ſcarcely One to Ten of the other Dramatiſts, as appears from *Athenæus*, and *Lilius Gyraldus.* Now, why were the Comick and Tragick Poets thus over-proportioned to the *Mimographi*, but becauſe their Entertainments were much more frequented and eſteemed than the other ? *nam & Pantomimus & Choraules in Comædia Canebant.*

Thirdly, It does not appear that the *Mimi* were always more Scandalous Compoſitions than Comedy. 'Tis true we have little of this kind of Writing remaining ; But by thoſe Fragments preſerv'd by *Macrobius*, and cited by *Lilius Gyraldus*, they ſeem to have been Modeſt and Sententious. And *Plinius Junior* mentioning *Vergilius Romanus*, another *Mimiiambick* Poet, commends him for *Macrob. Lib. 2. Saturn. cap. 7. Gyrald. de Poet. Hiſt. Dial. 8. P. 918*

for his Probity and his Wit, but does not
in the leaft tax him with any Indecency.
Befides, *Scaliger* in his Chapter *De Salta-
tione*, informs us, That the Dances proper
to the *Mimi* were Apifh and Fantaftical ;
but that feveral belonging to Comedy had
a Wanton and Licentious Movement. So
that of the Two, one would think thefe
Farces were fometimes the more inoffenfive
Performances.

Scalig. Poct.
Lib. 1. cap. 18.
p. 61, 64.

Fourthly, 'Tis certain that the *Mimes* and
Pantomimes Reprefented Comedy and Tragedy in their Geftures, and Dances, as well
as they did the *Mimi* or *Farces* properly fo
call'd. That the *Pantomimes* were concern'd
in the *Drama*, is plain from *Caffiodorus, &c.*
who tells us, That they could form
their Geftures into fuch a fignificancy,
that with the fame Limbs and Features
they could Act either *Hercules*, or *Venus* ;
and make the Paffions and Character of
of a King, or a Common Soldier, vifible
in their Poftures, and Motions. Now
Kings and Heroes, we know, were only
counted proper for Tragedy.

Macrob.Saturn.
Lib. 2.cap. 10.

Gyraldus, p.
690. de Dial.
6.

Indeed thefe fort of Actors were nothing
but *Mimicks*, (tho much farther improv'd
than the Moderns) and therefore as proper
to appear in the *Drama* as in any other
Stage-Performance. From whence it will
follow, that if thefe *Pantomimi's* were foul
in their Geftures, the *Drama* muft anfwer
to the Indictment ; It being oftentimes
only

only the Busineſs of theſe *Mimicks* to ſup-
ply the place of the Dialogue, and expreſs
the Paſſions of the Poem.

And thus I have plainly prov'd, that
when the Fathers paſs Sentence againſt the
Stage, the whole Myſtery and Fraternity is
included, ſo that his Diſtinction between
the *Drama,* and the *Mimi* and *Pantomimi,*
will do him no ſervice. And this may
ſerve to make good not only the Teſtimony
of *Clemens Alexandrinus,* but of the reſt of
the Fathers, all his Objections againſt the
Strength of their Evidence turning moſtly
upon this Suppoſition. But becauſe he
ventures to attack but Two Citations more,
a little farther Conſideration of him will
be no great matter.

I obſerv'd from *Theophilus Antiochenus,* that
the *Chriſtians durſt not ſee the Heathen Shews upon the account of their Indecency and Profaneneſs,*
and particularly that *the Stage-Adulteries of
the Gods and Hero's were unwarrantable Entertainments,* &c. Here he is poſitive that the
Tranſlator very well knew, that Tragedy & Comedy P. 28.
were unconcern'd and nothing but the Mimi *aim'd
at.* Say you ſo? Is not the *Drama* concern'd in
ſuch Repreſentations as theſe ? What do
you make of *Plautus's Amphytrio,* and *Terence's Eunuchus,* of *Euripides's* and *Seneca's
Thyeſtes,* not to mention any more? Here the
Adulteries of the Gods and Hero's are deſcrib'd
and acted, and in ſome of them make part
of the main Argument : And beſides all
this

ἁγιστεὶ μοι-
χείας παῤ αυ-
Τοῖς τραγω-
δεῖται.
Nihil nobis
cum impudici-
tia Theatri,&c.
Tertul. Apol.
cap. 38.
Ancient and
Modern Stage
survey'd, p 30.

this, the Expression throws it upon the *Drama.*

His next Complaint against me is for translating *Theatrum* a *Play-house :* This he very shrewdly calls *my old way of Legerdemain ;* for by all means it should have been rendred *Theatre.* I have a fine time on't to write against a Man that does not know what is Latin for a *Play-house !* Truly this is a great Point ! But I hope *Horace's* Authority may satisfie him, that his *Drama's* were Acted in the *Theatre.* Now this

Horat. Carm.
Lib. 2. Od. 1.

Poet addressing to *Pollio ,* desires him to stop his Tragick *Muse* till the Commonwealth was better settled :

Paulum severæ Musa Tragediæ
Desit Theatris.

P. 30.

The *Surveyor* goes on with his Grievances, and pretends that I wrest *Tertullian's* Words, and *force him to call* Pompey's *Theatre a Dramatick Bawdy-house.* And here he has very honestly again put the Latin in the Margin to confute the English : Thither I appeal, and doubt not but the Reader will find the *Original* every jot as severe as the *Translation.* But he complains the State of the Case *is chang'd,* the Drama *wrongfully accus'd,* and that *Tertullian inveigh'd only against the Shews of the* Mimi. That's strange ! Were not Comedies and Tragedies Acted in the Theaters ? Not in

Itaque Pompei-
us magnus, solo
Theatro suo mi-
nor, cum illam
arcem omnium
turpitudinum
extruxisset,
&c. Tertul. de
Spectac.cap 10.

Pom-

Pompey's Theatre, the moſt Magnificent in *Rome ?* Were Farces ſo much preferr'd to the *Drama*, and the Nobleſt Buildings contriv'd only for Drolls, and Strollers ? *Tertullian*, in this very Paragraph, obſerves, that the *Theatre* was Dedicated to *Bacchus* ; and this Idol, the *Surveyor* himſelf informs us, *was the Patron of the* Drama, P. 9. *and had his Altar on the right-ſide of the Stage.* Beſides, 'tis further evident that *Tertullian* levell'd his Cenſure againſt the *Drama* (for ſo I muſt call it) by the Caution he gives; he warns the Chriſtians not to be ſurpriz'd by ſome of the beſt-complexion'd Entertainments. *Look,* ſays he, *upon all the engaging Sentences of the Stage, their Flights of Fortitude and Philoſophy, the Loftineſs of the Stile, and the Fineneſs of the Conduct, &c. Look upon it only as Honey dropping from the Bowels of a Toad, or the Bag of a Spider.* Now I ſuppoſe the *Surveyor* is not ſo hardy as to affirm, That Heroick Fortitude, Lofty Expreſſion, and Moral Sentences, is any way ſuitable to his Deſcription of the Mimi. 'Tis plain therefore, that Comedy and Tragedy muſt be ſtruck at in the Teſtimony above mention'd.

Omnia illic ſeu fortia, ſeu honeſta, ſeu ſonora, ſeu ſubtilia proinde habe ac ſi ſtillicidia mellis de Libacunculo venenato, &c. De Spectac. cap. 27.

I muſt not forget the *Surveyor's* Suggeſtion, That the *Idolatry of the Stage* was the principal Quarrel the Fathers had againſt it. 'Twas for this Reaſon that they de- P. 13. *claim'd againſt it with all their Nerves and Vehe-*

Vehemence, as our Author words it. The
See *View,* &c.
Chap. 6.
Defence, &c.
p. 84. Reader may pleafe to take notice, that
the Fathers had other Reafons for their
Averfion to the Stage, befides the Charge
of Idolatry : However, upon this Occafion I fhall purfue the Argument a little
farther, and anfwer, Firft, That the Fathers were no lefs Enemies to Immorality
than to Falfe Worfhip. Indeed, one great
Reafon why *Paganifm* was fo very Cri-
minal, was, becaufe 'twas not only an er-
roneous, but a fcandalous Belief : 'Twas
becaufe the Holy Solemnities were Lewd,
and not only mif-led Men's Underftand-
ings, but debauch'd their Practice. Now
nothing in Nature is fo counter to Chriftianity as Wickednefs. Idolatry may
fometimes be an effect of Ignorance ; but
Immorality lies always open to Confcience
and inward Reproof. So that where Vice
is cherifh'd, and Licentioufnefs is made
creditable, there the worft Part of Heathenifm is kept up. The Devil is no lefs really Worfhipp'd in Lewdnefs and Obfcenity
than he was in *Venus* and *Jupiter.* And yet
the *Surveyor* has the Courage to affirm,
That *Idolatry is more abhorr'd and expos'd
on the Englifh Stage than any where elfe.* Idolatry expos'd ! What, by burlesking the
Bible, by Smut and Swearing, and by hoot-
ing, as much as in them lies, all Religion
out of the Univerfe ? A moft admirable
Expedient ! Thus Error is cur'd by A-
theifm,

theifm, and falfe Religion deftroy'd, by leaving no Truth to counterfeit!

The *Surveyor* obferves, That the *Fathers were alarm'd* at the Heathen *Stage* as at the Approach of an Enemy ; they were afraid the indulging thefe Liberties would hazard the Intereft and Belief of Chriftianity: *They juftly apprehended, that from a Liking of* P. 18. *the Entertainments, they might proceed to approve the Occafion of them.* Now thofe who frequent the Theatres, would do well to confider this Caution : For from liking the *Plays,* they may come to like the *Practice,* and flide infenfibly from the Diverfion to the Vice and Profanenefs. I wifh this Reafoning were not too well grounded upon Experiment ; but nothing is more natural than the Tranfition from Pleafure to Imitation. And thus the Fathers Reftraint holds ftrong againft the *Englifh* Theatre. For Lewdnefs is more catching than Heathenifm ; and People are much fooner furpriz'd by their Appetites, than by their Ignorance. 'Twas this Indulgence to Senfuality which captivated the World, P. 19. and gain'd Credit and Authority to Paganifm. Thus Vice gives the main Force to the Temptation, makes way for Error, and by corrupting the Will betrays the Underftanding. And this may ferve to fatisfie the *Reader* , that his Topick of Idolatry is nothing to the purpofe.

Upon

Upon the whole ; Let us suppose, which is not true, That the Fathers left *Comedy* and *Tragedy* uncensur'd, and planted their Rhetorick against nothing but the *Shews* of the *Mimi* ; let us resign our Advantage, and set part of our Evidence aside ; What would the *Surveyor* gain by it ? Alas ! unless he can clear the Innocence, and take off the Imputations upon the *English* Stage ; which he never so much as attempts : Unless this can be done, his Cavils and his Confidence, and all his other Pretences signifie nothing. For, can we imagine the Fathers would ever have endur'd the Disorders of the Modern Stage? Would these Holy Men have allow'd them their *Common Places* of Smut, and their Sallies of Profaneness ? Would they have seen Lewdness a Profession, and Religion made sport with, and said nothing against it ? No : Such flaming Provocations as these would have kindled their Spirits, and pressed them to the Encounter: Their Satyr would have thundred, and their Discipline been play'd against the Enemy ; and the Warnings of the Pulpit would have sounded as loud as the Blasphemies of the Play-house : Where the Honour of God and the Interests of Eternity suffered so much, they would have shewn a proportionable Concern. For like the Hero's in *Æschylus*, upon such an Occasion,

Σι διης

Σιδηνεύφρων (γὰρ) θυμὸς ἀνδρεία φλέγων
Ἔπνει λεόντων ὡς ἄρην δεδορκότων.

Æschyl. septem
contr. Thebas.

Brave in their Zeal, and fir'd with Resolution,
They look'd like Lions roaring to the Combat !

The *Surveyor* is tired with Church-An-
tiquity, for it seems all *my Translations of* P. 32.
the Fathers are of the same Stamp with those
he has Examined : Why, so they are; but
not a jot to his purpose. For notwithstanding all his Clamour about
my *Corrupt Version, Managing of Evidence,* P. 28. 33.
and what not; he has not been able to
shew that I have either mistaken the Sence,
or misapplied the Meaning in the least Instance; so that if *my main Strength,* as he
is pleased to say, *lay in these Worthies,* the
Forces are still entire, there is not so much
as a Vein scratch'd, or a drop of Blood
lost in the Encounter.

But I can't forget his Character and Com-
mendations of the *Fathers.* What would
you think *St. Cyprian, St. Chrysostome, St. Augustine,* and the rest of them were like ?
Why it seems they are *like Whelps newly*
enter'd, they run Riot, have much better Mouths P. 32.
than Noses; make up a great part of the Cry, but
are of no service in the Chase. Nay, then he
may well go on with t'other Compli- Ibid.
ment, and tell us, *Their Writings are*
but the Rubbish of Antiquity. Bless us !
What

What strains of Contempt and Distraction are here! Is this all that's due to the Memory of these Venerable Men? And must Dignity and Merit be thus coarsly Treated? Must Dogs and Martyrs be coupled, and Patriarchs describ'd by Similitudes from the *Kennel?* These great *Defenders* of the *Faith* were never saluted in this manner before: Jews and Heathens, tho they might have had no less Malice, had (as far as it appears) more Modesty than this comes to. One would think he learned this Language at the *Olympicks* (as he calls them) of *Moor-Fields*, or rather at the Great House that fronts them. If the *Fathers* are thus despicable, why does he follicit for their Votes, and strive to bring them over to his Party? If he takes them for his Friends, he uses them very severely; But I suppose he despairs of their Favour, and would therefore disable their Credit. Well; since the Fathers are thus unmanageable, and won't be tamper'd with, 'tis time to leave them: If the *Christians* won't do, we must try if the *Heathens* will prove any kinder. The *Surveyor* therefore applying to the *Philosophers*, endeavours to bribe them into Silence, and bring them to a State of Neutrality. But here he is much as untoward in his Objections as formerly. He pretends *Plato does not appear in his own Person:* Granting that, *Eusebius* is a good Voucher for

P. 34.

for his Opinion. But after all, *Plato* does *View,* p. 354.
appear in his own Perſon, and ſtands fairly
quoted in the Margin. Truly I think I'm
ſomewhat to blame for troubling my ſelf
with an Author ſo very Defective either in
Eyes or Honeſty. But it ſeems the Teſtimony
is not full to the Purpoſe. Why ſo? let's
hear it. *Plays* (ſays *Plato*) *raiſe the Paſſions,*
and pervert the Uſe of them, and by conſequence
are dangerous to Morality. This I take it is to
the Point; the Impeachment runs high,
and the Articles are plainly mention'd. So
that to evade the Force of the Authority, by
ſaying *the Nature or Meaſure of the Danger is* *Surv.* p. 35.
not ſpecified, is not to Argue, but Trifle, and
is in effect to make Blots inſtead of Letters
with a Man's Ink. My Buſineſs in the *View,*
&c. was to ſum up the Evidence in few
Words, and not to tire the Reader with un-
neceſſary Lengths of Quotation: However,
ſince he calls for't, I'll give it him ſomewhat
more particularly. 'Tis *Plato*'s Opinion then, *Plat. de Repub.*
that *the Diverſions of the Stage are dangerous to* lib. 10. p.756.
Temper and Sobriety; they ſwell Anger and De- Ed. Franc.,
ſire too much. Tragedy is apt to make Men boiſte-
rous, and Comedy Buffoons. Thus thoſe Paſſions are
cheriſh'd which ought to be check'd, Virtue loſes
ground, and Reaſon grows precarious.

From *Plato* we muſt go to *Xenophon:* And
here his Exception is, That *the Drama is* *Surv.* p. 35.
not mention'd. I grant it: But does not this
Author commend the *Perſians* for *not ſuffer-* *View,* &c. p.
ing their Youth to hear any thing Amorous or Taw- 234.
dry?

dry ? And does he not shew the Danger of such a Permission ? And is this nothing to the *English Stage*, where Love and Indecencies are most of the Entertainment ? This Remark not only reaches the *Modern*, but likewise the *Ancient Dramatists*, as far as their Compositions were any way licentious. At last the *Surveyor* owns, That *Bawdry was indeed forbidden to be talk'd to young People in* Persia, *because of the Heat of the Climate*. Meaning, that in the *Latitude* of *London* the case is otherwise: The Elevation of the *Pole* has taken off the Restraint, and made Modesty unnecessary : For in these Northern Regions, and especially in a hard Winter, Smut is a very harmless Diversion, and a Man may talk as Brutishly as he pleases!

Surveyor, p. 36.   He is now advanced to *Aristotle*, *whose Authority*, he says, *will do me as great Service as the Two former*. Now tho' this Jest is a good Answer to all that he offers in earnest, yet possibly he may take it ill, if his Story is not heard out. He objects then, That

View, p. 234 the Passage cited by the *View* from *Aristotle*, *amounts to no more than a General Caution against trusting Youth in promiscuous Company !* To this it may be answered,

   First, Aristotle plainly forbids young People the sight of *Comedy*, as appears even by the

Surveyor, p. 37. Latin Translation cited by the *Surveyor : Comœdiarum spectatores esse Lex prohibeat.* This is something more *than* a General Caution against *promis-*

promiscuous Company : For let the Reason of the
Prohibition be what it will, the *Drama* is
particularly ftruck at, and made counter-
band Goods to one Part of Human Life at
leaft. However, I did ill to *palm the general
Term of Debauchery , for· the particular one of*
Drunkennefs, which it feems *was only inftanc'd
in by the Philofopher.* Here the Tranflation
comes hard upon him again ; for not only
Drunkennefs is mention'd, but all the Diforders confequent upon it. And is not
Lewdnefs oftentimes the Effect of Intempe-
rance, efpecially in young People?

 Secondly, The *Greek* is ftill more unkind to
the *Surveyor,* and fhews that he has quite
miftaken *Ariftotle's* Sence ; which in a literal
Verfion runs thus: 'The Government fhould
'not permit Youth to fee Comedies, till Dif-
'cipline has fecured them from the Impref-
'fions and Mifchief of fuch Diverfions, and
'they are advanc'd to the Age of being ad-
'mitted to Feafts and Publick Entertainment.
This Tranflation is warranted by the Original and by *Heinfius's* Paraphrafe, and ju-
ftifies the *View* to the full. And now his
other Objection about my mifreprefenting
Ariftotle, being founded upon his former
Miftake, muft fall together with it.

 But the *Surveyor* and Mr. *Dennis* think it
ftrange, that *Ariftotle fhould* pronounce thus un-
*kindly upon Comedy, and yet leave Rules for the
Writing this kind of Poem.* Why this, if we
confi-

C 2

Margin notes:

P. 37.

*Vel ebrictatis,
vel aliarum
inde nafcentium
rerum incommo-
dis difciplina
liberos efficiat.
Τὰς ἢ νεωτε-
ρὰς ὔτε κωμω-
δίας διατάς
νομοϑετηον.
πρὶν ἢ την ἡλι-
κίαν λάβωσιν
ἐν ἢ ᾧ κατα-
κλίσεώς ὑπορ-
ξει κοινω νεῖν
ἤδη ᾧ μέϑην
ᾧ τῆς ἀπὸ τῶν
τιὔτων γιγ ο-
μένης βλάβ. ᾳ
ἀπαϑεῖς ἡ παι-
δεία ποιήσει.
Arift. Polit. lib.
7. cap. 17. Ed.
Lugd. Batav.*

*Surveyor, p. 36.
Dennis, p. 74.*

consider it, is no great Mystery : Plays are
one thing in the abstracted Idea, and another
in Fact and Practice : He might dislike the
common Liberties of the Poets, without ab-
solutely condemning the Form of them. But
that *Aristotle* did not allow of Licentious
Comedy, is plain by the Instance before us,
View, &c. by what I cited elsewhere in the *View*, and
p. 160. by his Advice to Governours , *to banish*
Polit. lib. 7. *Smut and Indecency from the Common-wealth.*
cap 17.
View, p. 235, *Tully's* Testimony comes next to be examined, who, as I observed, cries *out upon*
licentious Plays and Poems, as the Bane of So-
briety and wise Thinking : That Comedy subsists
upon Lewdness, and that Pleasure is the Root of
all Evil. This one would imagine were
pretty home : What does the *Surveyor* say to
it ? Is the Testimony miscited ? Not at all.
Surveyor, p.42. What then ? Why *these Sentences are Ends*
and Scraps of Authors, and as little to the pur-
pose as if he had cited so many Propositions out
of Euclid, *which tho' true, are of no use in this*
place. No! Is *Tully's* Censure of Licentious
Plays, affirming that Comedy subsists upon
Lewdness, and that Pleasure is the Root of
all Evil ; is all this nothing to the purpose ?
This is raging Impertinence ; I almost sweat
to take notice of such stuff as this is. As
for his calling what I produc'd *Scraps*, I must
tell him, 'twas not for want of Plenty that
I gave him no more ; however, till he can
get this off his Stomach, he has no reason to
complain of Scarcity. The Reader , if he
please,

pleafe, may fee a whole Page of Declamation to the fame purpofe ; at the latter end of which he has thefe Words: * *Thefe Poets are great Affiftances to Virtue, and we have rea-fon to expect moft admirable Cures from the Stage! Yes ! Manners muft be mightily reformed by thofe People who make Love and Lewdnefs a Deity, and teach Men to worfhip their own Folly and Diftraction ! I fpeak (fays he) of Comedy, which were it not for fuch licentious Management could go on no longer. This Paffage is quoted by the *Surveyor*, according to his cufto-mary Policy: He is refolv'd I perceive to make fure Work on't, and to confute him-felf, for fear it fhould be done by fome body elfe. But if the cafe ftands thus, the *Sur-veyor* is pofitive, that *either* Tully *or* Mr. Col-lier *are extreamly miftaken.* This is manfully put, I confefs ; but I'm afraid 'twon't do : For if *Tully* fhould be miftaken, which is very unlikely, it would fignifie little ; for 'tis not the Reafoning, but the Authority of *Tully* which is now in queftion. Then as for my felf, I can't be *miftaken,* unlefs the Citation is falfe, which he does not fo much as offer to difprove. He objects farther, That *Plau-tus* and *Terence are the only Comedians remain-ing, from whom we can form any Judgment of the* Roman *Comedy, before or about* Cicero's *time ; but thefe* Mr. Collier *affures us are mo-deft to a Scruple, efpecially* Terence. To this I anfwer,

* *O præclaram emendatricem vitæ Poeticam, quæ amorem flagitii, & le-vitatis aucto-rem, in concilio Deorum collo-candum putet ! De Comedia lo-quor quæ fi hæc flagitia non probaremus nul-la fffet omnino.* Tufc. Queft, Lib. 4.

Surv. p. 40.

Ibid.

Firft,

First, That what I affirm'd of the Modesty of *Terence*, was in reference to his Language, not to his Matter or Argument, which is sometimes exceptionable enough to draw the Censure of *Tully* upon him. Then as to *Plautus*, I introduc'd him with a Mark of Dislike, and only commended him upon the Parallel with the *English* Stage. Now where's the Contradiction of all this ? May not Men be very much to blame, without being the worst of their Kind? Here's room enough then for *Cicero*'s Reprimand of *Plautus* and *Terence*, without doing the *View* the least disservice. But,

Secondly, *Plautus* and *Terence* are not the *only Poets from whom we can take any measure of the* Roman *Comedy about* Cicero's *time :* For in the very place *Tully* cites several Verses from *Trabea* and *Cæcilius* ; and blames these Comick Poets for magnifying Love-Adventures, making *Cupid* a God, and flourishing too much upon the Satisfactions of Sense ; tho' nothing of this was done with the Modern Grosness. This Passage being in the same place with that quoted by the *Surveyor*, he must needs see it : From whence the Reader may observe how nicely he keeps up to his usual Exactness. Farther, *Tully* does not only complain of Comedy, but of Tragedies too. He blames them for *representing their Hero's impatient under Misfortune ; such Instances of Weakness and Discomposure were* , in his Opinion, *of dangerous Example :* So that let but the

Stage

Tusc. Quæst.
lib. 4.

Tusc. Quæst.
lib. 2.

Stage (fays he) *ftrike in with the Prejudices of Education, and this is enough to baffle the Force of Virtue ; and cut the very Sinews of Fortitude.*

The *Surveyor*, at the Head of his Remarks upon this Teftimony, brightens his Air, and would feem to look kindly upon Modefty : But this Smile, tho' unufual, appears angry and difturb'd. *He fuppofes no one will defend licentious Plays ; but if fome warm-headed Enthufiaftick Zealot pretends to find fome Paffages really guilty, they are willing to give them up.* This is the only Paffage in his Book, as I remember, in which he drops the leaft Word againft Lewdnefs : But then he touches the Point very tenderly, clogs the Cenfure with a great many kind Provifo's, * and is ftrangely out of Humour with thofe *Enthufiaftick Zealots* that make any Difcovery. And to make all fure, he lays in for *Countenance and Encouragement to the prevailing Merit of the main Part of the Performance.* For Example, if an Apothecary mixes up Poifon with a Receipt, yet if it does not weigh as much in the Scale as the reft of the Ingredients, all is well enough, and the *prevailing Merit* of the Dofe, tho' it murthers the Patient, ought to be *encourag'd.*

Livy's Authority comes after *Tully*, and muft be confidered. This *Evidence*, fays the *Surveyor*, comes *not near our Cafe*, were the Credit on't unexceptionable. His Reafon is becaufe *Livy fpeaks of Stage Reprefentations in*

Surv. p. 39.

* *Ibid.*

Ibid.

Survey, p. 44.

gene-

general, but the Drama *was not known amongst
the* Romans *at this time when the* Ludi Scenici
were invented. I'le try to make an Argument
like this. For Inftance : The City built upon Seven Hills, and upon the *Tyber*, was by
no means *Rome* in the time of *Tarquinius
Prifcus* ; Why fo ? Why, becaufe tho it
ftood upon the fame Ground, it was not near
fo big as 'twas afterwards in the Reign of
Auguftus. But for all this fine Reafoning,
effe and *bene effe* are Notions of the fame Subject.
'Tis true, things are not always perfected at
their firft Invention ; but I thought the Fi-
nifhing and Improvement they might afterwards receive, would not alter them in their
Name and Nature. And as to the Bufinefs
in hand, I have already fhewn, that *Comedy*
and *Dancing*, and all the Diverfions of the
Stage, were perform'd together at firft : And
that the *Drama* and the *Ludi fcenici* were the
fame, I fhall take for granted at prefent, and
afterwards prove it by the *Surveyor's* Authority, and by St. *Auguftine's* too, who mentioning the Original of *Plays*, explains himfelf exprefly in *Comedy*, and *Tragedy.* De
Civit. Dei Lib. 2. cap. 8. His next Undertaking is to Quarrel with the *Tranflation :* To
clear this the Hiftorian muft be cited. Now
Livy giving an Account of the Original of
Plays, affigns this Reafon for the Relation ;
Dec. 1. Lib. 7. *Ut appareat quam ab fano initio res in hanc vix
opulentis regnis tolerabilem infaniam venerit.* He
affirms the Original of Plays were commen-
dable,

dable, becaufe they were brought in upon
the fcore of Religion; and to remove a
Mortality. This being thus reported by *Livy*,
I Tranflated the Paffage above-mentioned as
follows; *That the Motives are fometimes good,* View, p. 235.
when the Means are ftark naught. And where's
the Miftake of this rendring? Don't the
Words of the Author, and the Confequence
of the Practice, plainly juftifie the Conftruction? Nay, his own Interpretation makes
his Objection unreafonable. For he Tran-
flates *Vix tolerabilem infaniam, &c.* An ex- Survey, p. 45,
ceffive extravagance which fcarce the Wealthieft 46.
Nation can bear. Now if the *Profufion at thefe*
Shews were ready to break the Back of the
Roman Empire, had not I reafon for faying
in the Verfion, *That the Means were ftark*
naught, and the Remedy worfe than the Difeafe?
But this puts me in mind of another Difference to be adjufted. The *Surveyor* contends,
That *Livy* in this place *does not condemn the Im-*
morality, but the Luxury, and Profufion at thefe
Shews. The *Luxury* of thefe Diverfions, if
it muft be call'd fo, I fuppofe confifts in o-
ver-pleafing a Vitious Palate; But let that
pafs. The *Surveyor* fupports his Conjecture
from the Citations adding, That this *Infa-*
nia, or Diforder, *was greater than the Wealthieft*
Nations * *could well bear.* Now fays the *Surveyor,* * *Vix opulenti-*
Wealthy People have as much need of Morality *regnis tolerabi-*
as the Poor. No doubt on't; and are in more *lem.*
danger too of mifcarrying in that Matter.
For, as my Adverfary has obferved, a Na-

Survey, p. 12. tion is too apt to *grow Wealthy*, and *Wanton* together : This made *Saluſt* complain, *That the Riches of the* Roman *Empire occaſioned the Decay of Diſcipline, and the Diſſolution of Manners.* Without Care, People's Virtue, I mean their Sobriety, is apt to ſink with the Riſe of their Fortunes ; Their Appetites for Liberty are more awaken'd by Opportunity and Temptation : They have more Money to purchaſe their Pleaſures, and more Leiſure to enjoy them. And beſides, ſuch Circumſtances are farther within the danger of Flattery, and ill Example ; 'Tis no wonder therefore to hear *Livy* affirm, That a Government almoſt overgrown with Wealth and Power, ſhould be in greater danger of Playhouſe Infection, then when they were Poor, and more ſlenderly eſtabliſh'd : For then their Neceſſities were ſome Security ; They could not go to the Expence of Vice, nor had ſo much time to be Debauch'd.

Secondly, That *Livy* by *this Diſtraction*,
* Inſania.* meant Licentiouſneſs, will appear by his Cenſure of the *Stage* in another place, which we ſhall come to by and by.

The *Surveyor* rages mightily about my Miſtranſlating the following part of the Teſti-
Cum piaculorum magis conquiſitio animos, quam corpora morbi inficerent.mony, which runs thus : *The Remedy in this caſe is worſe than the Diſeaſe, and the Atonement more infectious than the Plague.* Here I confeſs my Edition miſlead me, which, (as I remember, for I have loſt the Book) has *inficerent*, inſtead of *afficerent*, tho I muſt own

own this latter Reading appears the beſt. But notwithſtanding this accident the Surveyor ſhall be no loſer, for *Livy* ſhall make it up to him another way. And not to defer his Satisfaction, this Hiſtorian informs us, *That when a Theatre was building by the Cenſors Direction*, Scipio Naſica *ſpoke againſt it in the* Houſe, *as a Uſeleſs and Debauching Experiment, and got an Act for the pulling it down.* Here *Livy* not only pulls down the Playhouſe, but gives ſuch a Reaſon for the doing it, that one would think ſhould have kept it in Rubbiſh ever after. And if he queſtions the Authority of *Livy's Epitome*, *Sigonius*, not to mention *Voſſius*, may ſatisfie him; who delivers his Opinion in theſe Words; *Nam ſive a Livio, ſive a Floro, ſive ab alio quo ſcriptæ ſunt, (hæc enim omnia Traduntur) ad Romanas certe res illuſtrandas accommodatiſſimæ ſunt, præſertim vero ubi Liviana Hiſtoria excidit. Qua in parte Livianam apud quemque obtinere debent auctoritatem. Sigon. Schol. p. 6.*

Quum locatum à Cenſoribus Theatrum extrueretur, p... Cornelio Naſica auctore tanquam inutile, & nociturum publicis moribus, ex Senatus conſulto deſtructum eſt. Liv. Lib. 48. in Epit.

We muſt now proceed to the Teſtimony of *Valerius Maximus*; And here the Surveyor will make ſufficient Amends for being ſomewhat in the Right before. This Teſtimony he affirms relates to the *Arena*, and concerns none but the *Gladiators* and *Cæſtiarii*: And then very liberally again quotes his own Confutation in the Margin: * In earneſt does this Critick not underſtand the difference between *Theatres*, and *Amphitheatres*, and that the firſt were for *Plays*,

* Ad Theatra gradus faciendus eſt. —— Religionem civili ſanguine Scenicorum Portentorum gratia maculârunt. Valer. Max. Lib. 2. Cap. 4. Survey. p. 47.

Plays, and the latter for *Prizes ?* A little School-Learning would have set him right in this Matter, and likewise prevented the Misfortune of making *Scenica portenta* signifie *Gladiators ;* which I think has more of prodigy in the *Translation,* than in the Etymology and Story. And now I suppose it may be pretty plain, that either the *Surveyor* does not understand *Latin,* or is not fit to be trusted with it. Farther, the *Surveyor's* Mistakes are the more unpardonable, because *Valerius Maximus* spends almost this whole Chapter in describing the Rise and Progress of *Plays,* the Buildings and Decorations of the *Theatre,* together with the Checks they received from the Government. He tells us in the very second Paragraph, *That these Play-houses were begun by* Messalla, *but stop'd by* Scipio Nasica, *who sold all their Materials by the Common Cryer. And that the Senate made a Law, that there should be no Seats or Benches for the Audience to see Plays at within a Mile of the Town.* This Passage is expresly cited by St. *Augustine,* and hinted by *Tertullian,* to shew how much the Play-house was discouraged by the *Roman* Magistracy.

As to the *Animosæ acies* which he would fain wrest to the *Prizes* in spight both of the *Latin* and History of his Author, they are to be understood of the *Quarrels* and Bloodshed which were not very uncommon at the *Play-house,* as *Tacitus* informs us.

Fer

Quæ (i. e. *Theatra*) *inchoata sunt a Messalla,* &c. Valer. Max. p. 156. Ed. Varior.

August. de Civ. Dei Lib. 1. *cap.* 33. *Tertull. de Spect. cap.* 10. *æ Theatrali licentia proxi- mo priore anno cæpta, gravius tum erumpit. occisis non modo e plebe,* &c. Tacit. Annal. Lib. 1. cap. 77.

For at one Riot, which was not the first, there
were several Burghers, Soldiers, a Captain, and
a Colonel of the Guards killed in the Fray. Now,
I hope, this Company may have more Roman
Blood * in their Veins, and may better stand
for the State in the Translation, than his
Rabble of Gladiators, who were generally
Slaves and Malefactors. To return to Tacitus, This Tumult, as he goes on, was brought
before the Senate, where the Actors had like to
have come under a very ignominious Discipline :
In short, the Playhouse had some Regulations
put upon it, and the Disorders of the Audience
were punished with no less than Banishment.
This happened in the Reign of Tiberius; Now
the Theatre continuing still out of order, and
some of the Magistracy having often complained of
it to no purpose, at last the Emperor himself moved
in the House, that the Lewdness and Riots of
these Diversions might be effectually suppressed :
Upon which the Players were banished out of
Italy.

There is part of Valerius Maximus his Testimony behind, in which, as I observed in
the View, he concludes the Consequences of Plays
intolerable, and that the Massilienses did well in
clearing the Country of them. Here the Surveyor
flies to his old Distinction between the Mimi
and the Drama, which having disabled already, I might reasonably call a new Cause;
but to give him farther satisfaction, I shall
prove, that the Stage is here meant in all its
Latitude and variety of Diversion.

*Sanguis ci-
vilis.
Surveyor, p. 48.*

*Actum de ea se-
ditione apud
patres, diceban-
turque senten-
tiae ut Praeto-
ribus jus
Virgarum in
Histriones es-
set, &c. Ibid.
Variis dehinc,
& saepe in ri-
tia Praetorum
questibus, po-
stremo Caesar de
immodestia Hi-
strionum ret-
tulit, &c.——
pulsi tum histri-
ones Italia.
Annal. Lib. 4.
cap. 14.*

View, p. 236.

Then

1. *Then* Valerius Maximus *in the beginning of the Paragraph, commends the Republick of Mar-seilles for the Sobriety of their Discipline, and keeping up to their ancient Customs* *. Now we are to observe, that the *Massilienses* were a Colony of the *Phocenses* in *Jonia*, who not being willing to submit to the *Persian* Government, quitted that Country, and settled in *Gaul*. Now this Removal was in the Reign of *Cyrus*, in the very Infancy of the Stage, when there was nothing but some rude beginnings of Tragedy at *Athens* ; Besides, the *Massilienses* came from *Phocis*, where neither *Aristotle* or *Lilius Gyraldus* mention any thing of the settling or Invention of the *Drama :* By consequence, if the *Massilienses* were so tenacious of their Original Customs, they could have no such thing as Tragedy and Comedy among them ; These Entertainments being, as far as it appears, posterior to the forming of their Commonwealth. This will appear farther, if we consider, that, as *Suetonius* observes, the Business of the *Mimicks* was Originally part of Comedy * ; so that let us suppose, which we can't grant, that the *Drama* was as ancient as the Government of the *Massilienses*, and in use among them, yet we can't with any colour suppose, that the *Mimi* were distinct from *Comedy* at that time of day ; so that if the *Massilienses* were such Admirers of the first Plan of their Government, and stood off so nicely from all Innovation, they must

ex-

* *Prisci moris, observantia.* Val. Max. L. 2. cap. 6.

Lilius Gyrald. de poet. Hist. Dial. 6.

* *Vid. supra.*

exclude the *Drama* as well as the *Mimi*, otherwise the Form of their Stage would be changed, and their Customs receive an alteration.

2. The Reason *Valerius Maximus* gives, why the Inhabitants of *Marseilles* refused to admit this Entertainment, * agrees very well with the *Drama*, *It was because the Subject and Gross of these Diversions was mostly Intrigue and Debauchery : These Circumstances the Government were afraid might grow infectious, and spread from Fiction into Practice.* Now this is exactly the Description which *Tully* gives of Comedy, *which (says he) were it not for Amours and Lewdness, would have no Matter to proceed upon* * .

Nullum aditum in Scenam Mimis dando, &c. Quorum argumenta majore ex parte stuprorum continent actus, ne talia spectandi consuetudo, e-tiam imitandi licentiam sumat.L.2 cap.6.

* *Tusc. Quest. Lib. 4. vid. supra.*

3. The introductive Clause which leads to this Discountenance, points it clearly on the *Drama*. *The Massilienses* (says the Author) *were extreamly strict and severe in their Government and Administration* *. Now by the *Surveyor's* Account of the *Mimes* and *Pantomimes*, this could never be meant of them. For they, says he, Danced Naked, and were in their Gestures foul to the last Degree of Scandal. I would gladly know, what Instance of Severity it could be to deny Admission to such Monsters as these ? Is it indeed an Argument of extraordinary Rigour not to allow the grossest Liberties, and which had often been marked and punished at *Rome ?* A Government can't be said to be remarkably Rigid, unless they tie

* *Ea civitas severitatis custos acerrima est. Ibid. Surveyor, p. 24.*

up

up their Subjects to particular Restraints, and
bar them the Freedoms commonly practised
elsewhere. The *Massilienses* therefore having
this Character of Severity, it must be because they would not admit of the more
inoffensive Performances of the Stage; because they refused the Diversions of Comedy
and Tragedy, which were then generally
permitted in the *Roman* Empire.

4. *Mimus*, the Word which the *Surveyor*
cavils upon, is by other good Authors taken
for a *Play*, in the sence of the *Drama*, as
this Gentleman loves to speak. Thus the
Learned *Thysius* upon the place understands
it. The Massilienses, (says he) *cleared their
Country of* Comedy, *and all sorts of* Stage-
Plays. This they did because they looked
upon them as the Nurseries of Lewdness.
And *Suetonius* tells us, That *Augustus* being
at the point of Death, ask'd some of his
Friends, *Ecquid iis videretur mimum vitæ com-
mode transegisse*. Now I would ask the *Surveyor* what he thinks of this Matter? Did
the Emperor enquire whether he had been a
good *Pantomime* in his Life? Whether he
had acted like a finish'd Debauchee, and been
Lewd without Shame or Measure? Did *Augustus* affect such a Character as this, or think
his Memory would be obliged by it? Such
a Supposition would be a Libel upon *Nero*,
who when he came to dye had the Justice to
be displeased with his own Lewdness.

*Itaque Come-
diam omnesque
adeo Scenicos
Ludos Republica
sua ejecerunt;
Videbant enim
eam esse lasci-
viæ matrem
nequitiæ ma-
gistram, &c.
Thysius in Loc.
Sueton. in
August.*

The

The meaning therefore of this Queſtion of *Auguſtus* muſt be, Whether he had behaved himſelf well in his Station, and acted his Part handſomly, as a good *Player* does upon the *Stage* ; From whence it will follow, that *Mimus* muſt be taken for a *Play* in its uſual ſignification. But 'tis time to diſmiſs *Valerius Maximus,* and paſs on to *Seneca,* who it ſeems *has but little to ſay to the Matter.* He ſhould have ſaid, he has but little to ſay to *Seneca :* However, let the *View, &c.* decide that Queſtion. Well ! if *Seneca* ſays but little, he is reſolved to fortifie his Teſtimony, and help him out. For he frankly confeſſes, *That the* Roman *youth were generally corrupted by the Countenance which* Nero *gave to the Stage, and to all thoſe Arts which gratified and indulged the Senſes, and that this Philoſopher's Complaint was not unreaſonable.* Truly I think ſo too, or elſe I had never cited him. In this place the *Surveyor* is ſomewhat kinder than ordinary, for here he not only quotes, * but argues for me too, and gives me both *Text* and *Margin* to make my beſt of. This Knack of Writing and Recanting at the ſame time, is a good ſubtle Expedient : For if ever he ſhould be queſtioned for publiſhing a Book to Debauch the Nation, he can make ſubſtantial Proof he has confuted himſelf, and that it's to be hoped may ſtop the Proſecution. I muſt confeſs I like an Author that knocks his own Miſchief on the Head, and like the Scorpion is both Poyſon and Antidote.

Surveyor, p. 50.

View, &c. p. 236.

Surveyor, p. 50, 51.

* *Nihil vero tam damnoſum bonis moribus quam in aliquo ſpectaculo deſidere, tunc enim per voluptatem vitia facilius ſurrepunt. Senec. Epiſt. 7.* Survey, p. 51.

D

dote. But the *Surveyor* objects, That *Sene-*
ca's Charge againſt the *Shews* * is *general.*
Why then they are all comprehended :
Then he may be ſure the moſt remarkable
Shews, ſuch as the *Stage,* are concerned in the
Caution ; eſpecially ſince the Author has elſe-
where expreſly declaim'd againſt it. Well!
I perceive all this Skirmiſhing has nothing
but feint and falſe Alarm, but now he is reſolved to come to the Aſſault in good earneſt,
and enter upon the *Breach* of the Quotation,
for there, if you will believe him, I have *made*
a ſhift to ſteal in Two Falſifications. Now to try
this Cauſe, and diſcover the foul Play, we muſt
read the *Deed* in the Court. The Original runs
thus. *Tunc enim per voluptatem vitia facilius ſurre-*
punt. The Tranſlation thus : *For there Vice makes*
an inſenſible approach, and ſteals upon us in the Diſ-
guiſe of Pleaſure. * And where is the harm
of all this ? Harm! Why I have corrupted
one of the *Eight Parts of Speech,* and ſuborn'd
the *Adverb Tunc* to give in falſe Evidence, by
Tranſlating it *There,* inſtead of *Then.* Nay,
that's intolerable! For *Seneca,* you muſt obſerve, had nothing to ſay againſt the *Shews,*
and the *Play-houſe,* the Diverſion or the Company! The *Then,* the Circumſtance of Time
was the Bugbear ; All the infection lay in
the Clock, or the Sun-Dial : For People may
ſee what *Shews,* and go to what *Place* they
pleaſe, and be ſafe enough, provided they
do it at no *Time* ; This is exactly the *Sur-*
veyor's Reaſoning ; and thus he proves the
In-

* *Spectaculum,* p. 52.
View, p. 236.
* *View,* p.236.

Indictment. The next *Falsification* is my Surveyor, p. 53.
rendring the *words, Per Voluptatem,* in the
𝕯𝖎𝖘𝖌𝖚𝖎𝖘𝖊 𝖔𝖋 𝕻𝖑𝖊𝖆𝖘𝖚𝖗𝖊; For all that, if he
renders them otherwise, I'm satisfied he'l do
it worse. Indeed I think these Objections
are not made *in the Disguise* of Sence. To
conclude, if I was so unfair as *to steal in Two
Falsifications,* I had, it seems the Discretion
to steal them out again; for 'tis plain, there's
none of them to be found at present.

Tacitus and *Plutarch* appear next, and are
given up by him. But then he is never at
a loss, for when he can't Reason he can
Rail, and so the Book goes on as well as
ever.

I produced *Ovid* and Mr. *Wycherley* to shew
that the *Audience* at the Play-house was dangerous, as well as the Entertainment : A- Surv. p. 55.
gainst this the *Surveyor* insinuates, That if nothing but Solitude and Retirement will se-
cure us, we must not go to Church; for
there is mixt Company, and bad Designs
too sometimes. Under favour, this does not
follow. To go to Church is our Duty : Now
a Man's Business, and especially when Religious, is his Guard : And God will let no
Body miscarry for their Obedience. Besides,
the Quality of the Employment, the Solem-
nity of the Place, and the Majesty of the
Presence, is apt to furnish good Thoughts,
and check those which are otherwise.

But at the *Play-house* the Case is quite different : This is a Place where Thinking is

out

out of Doors, and Seriousness Impertinent. Here our Reason is apt to be surpriz'd, and our Caution disarm'd; Here Vice stands upon Prescription, and Lewdness claims Privilege to Solicit. Nay, the very Parade, the Gaiety, and Pleasure of the Company, is not without its danger: These Circumstances heightned with Luscious Dialogue, lively Action, and airy Musick, are very likely to make an unserviceable Impression. And thus we see our standing is but slippery, and the Tide runs high against *Flesh* and *Blood*: And as for the Protection of Heaven to bring us off, 'tis Presumption to expect it. If we will sit in the *Seat* of the *Scornfull*, and make Wickedness our Diversion, Providence we may be sure will withdraw, and leave us to the Government of another *Influence*.

To do the *Surveyer* Right, he is somewhat of my Opinion in this Matter. He *won't deny but a promiscuous conflux of People of all* *Ages, Sexes, and Conditions, will make the bu-* *siness of Intrigue go forward, and facilitate En-* *terprizes of this Nature.* But he is afraid, if a *Restraint* were laid upon People, and they were kept out of Harms way, it would be worse with them: And for the truth of this Conjecture, he appeals to the Experiment of *Italy*, and *Spain* ; where he observes there is a great deal of Care, and yet a great deal of Miscarriage. It may be so; but if they are bad under Caution, 'tis to be feared Liberty would never mend them. His reasoning about
the

Survey, p. 55, 56.

Ibid.

the *Imagination* being *vitiated* (*p.* 56.) for
want of Freedom is very slender, for Opportunity makes a Thief; The Temptation rises
upon sight, for Sence is stronger than Memory, and Life, than Painting. If the
strength of the Stream forces the Bank to
give way, the making the Breach wider, is
not, I suppose, the proper Method to stop
the Torrent. He had best perswade the
Dutch to pull up their Dikes and their Dams;
because in several Countreys where the *Sea*
is left to its Course, it does no manner of
damage. I confess I never heard that the
Spaniards and *Italians* were all Fools till now:
But it seems so 'tis with them : For they are
still perfect Strangers to themselves, and know
nothing of the Temper of their People, after
so many Ages for Information. But of all
Men, the *Surveyor* should not have been se-
vere upon the Reservedness of the *Spaniards*, *Surveyor, p.* 35.
because he had allowed it in the *Persians* be-
fore : His Reason was, because the *Heat of
the Climate, and the Warmth of their Constituti-
ons, hurried them very precipitiously* (as he Phrases
it) *into Irregularities.* Now *Spain* is as hot as
Persia; Why then all this Partiality ? That
that's Sawce for a Goose is Sawce for a
Gander. Why must the Poor *Spaniard* be
maul'd for his Caution, and for preventing
his Family from being *hurried very precipitiously
into Irregularities ?*

But

But after all, the *Caffres* and *Soldanians*, the Monſters of *Africk* both in Figure and Folly, and which, (as to ſome of them) whether Men or Munkeys, has been diſputed. Theſe *Æquinoctial* Sages are much Wiſer, it ſeems, in the Guard of Virtue, than the *Spaniards* and *Italians!* For *in many places under the Line, where the People go conſtantly naked, the familiarity of the Objects takes away all Wantonneſs of Imagination, which the artificial difficulties of ſome Countreys promote.* Say you ſo, muſt *Spain* and *Italy* be reformed by *Africk*, and brought up to the Standard of the *Line?* Muſt People go *naked* to ſecure their Modeſty? Theſe are wonderful Diſcoveries, and one would almoſt conclude by the drift of them, that the Man had a fancy to turn either *Adamite* or *Pantomime.* Theſe *Artificial Difficulties* of Cloaths ſpoil all: They diſſerve the Intereſt of Virtue, and are an Impolitick Contrivance. This fine Phraſe puts me in mind of his Quareling a Sentence of mine for want, as he pretends, of Syntax and Grammar: And therefore upon this occaſion I muſt tell him, That if the Charge was true, Sence without Grammar, is ſomewhat better then Grammar without Sence.

Ovid, by the *Surveyor's* Confeſſion, *pleads guilty, and owns not only the Opportunity, but the Buſineſs of the Place promotes Lewdneſs.* But then he fences againſt the Teſtimony with his uſual evaſion, and turns it all upon the *Repreſentation of the* Mimi: but the next Verſe

Surveyor, p. 56.

Survey, p. 57.

Verſe to that, in his *Margin*, will be ſufficient
to beat him off his Guard.

Ut tamen hoc fatear, Ludiquoque ſemina prebent De Triſt. Lib.2,
Nequitiæ tolli tota Theatra jube. View, 239.

Thus *Ovid* we ſee is for quite Levelling the
Enemies Works : He is for pulling down all
the *Play-houſes*, and not leaving ſo much
as a Corner of them ſtanding for *Comedy* and
Tragedy. This Line of the Poet had too much
Light to be look'd on, and therefore the *Surveyor* was reſolved to wink hard, and get
over it. There is another Verſe likewiſe in
the Citation ; which one would have thought
might have put him beſide the fancy of his View, p. 239.
Mimi ; and 'tis this, Ov. Remed,
Amor.

Quid caveat Actor, quid juvet arte docet.

This *Pentameter* refers much more to *Dialogue* than *Dancing*, to the Methods of Courtſhip, and the Myſteries of Intrigue, which
are generally the Subject of *Comedy*.

And now the *Surveyor* thinks fit to make a
Halt, and ſeems extreamly ſatisfied with his
performance : *I have*, ſays he, *at length run* P. 57,
*through all his private Authorities againſt the
Stage.* Run through them ! Yes, like a Bowl
that gets nothing ; or if you pleaſe, like a
Souldier that runs the Gauntlet. Indeed this
Author's Method is ſo very peculiar, he does
ſo often fall foul upon his own Book, quote

D 4 away

away his Argument, and mortifie himself, that one would almost fancy he wrote for a Pennance.

We are now coming up to the Censures of the *State*; Upon this Head I began with the *Athenians*, and observ'd, that this Republick *made a Law, that no Judge of the* Areopagus *should write a Comedy*. Here the *Surveyor* is *surpriz'd to find the* Athenians *produced against the* Drama, *of which they were the greatest Encouragers*. As great Encouragers as they were, their forbidding the Judges writing Comedy, proves they look'd upon't as the most unreputable part of Poetry. Now this was enough for my purpose. Nay, after a little struggling the *Surveyor* comes forward to a Compliance. He grants writing Comedy was likely to engage the Author *in Quarrels and Partialities, and was also an Indignity to the Office of a Judge*. And is not all this a sign, that there was something untoward and unreputable in the performance? His objecting, that *Aristophanes* had the better of *Socrates*, is no Argument of the standing Interest of Comedy: For 'tis pretty plain *Socrates* was oppress'd by a Faction, and executed in a Hurry: For soon after, the Government repented, his Memory was honour'd, and his Prosecutor *Melitus* Ston'd to Death. But after all, the *Surveyor's* being surpriz'd, 'tis no such News to find the *Drama* discountenanc'd at *Athens:* For he frankly

Marginal notes:
View, p. 240.

Survey, p. 58, 59.

Survey, p. 61.

Lilius Girald. de poet. Hist. Dial. 7. p. 780, 824.

frankly affirms, there was once a total sup-
preffion of it, an *abdication*, as he calls it, of *Survey*, p. 61.
Tragedy and Comedy : However I'm willing
to grant him the *Athenians* were none of the
worft *Friends to the* Stage ; I told him as much : *View*, p. 240.
But alafs, they paid for their fancy at laft ;
for the *Expence of this Diverfion, their Saunt-
ring at the* Playhoufe, *and minding Poets more
than Field Officers, was, as* Juftin obferves, *Juftin, Lib. 6.
fub. fin.*
*the Ruine of their Government : Thus Prodiga-
lity and Sloth made way for Slavery : And* Philip
of Macedon, *a little obfcure Prince, grew Mafter
of the Liberties of* Greece.

From *Athens* we muft Travel to *Sparta,*
where I obferved the *Stage was not allow'd un-* *View*, p. 240.
der any Form or Regulation. Here the *Surveyor*
grows angry, becaufe I gave the *Lacedemonians* a good Word, and after having faid
they were *fomewhat of my Kidney*, falls a rail- *Survey*, p. 64.
ing unmercifully upon them, and calls them
Cynical, Proud, and what not. Well ! Thefe
Cynicks, and he together, put me in mind of
old *Diogenes*, who trampled on *Plato's* Pride
with a greater of his own. I confefs the *Surveyor's* Satyr has fo much of the *Ruft* and
Roughnefs he declaims againft, that, I'm a-
fraid, he'l appear much more *unlick'd* (as he
has it) than *the Lacedemonian Laws.* But, by
this Gentleman's favour, I was far from o-
ver-flourifhing upon the 'partan's Character,
as appears fufficiently from *Plutarch*, to mention no other Author. ' This great Man
com-

' commends them for their Courage, their
' Difcipline, and their Sence ; declares, that
' he could not perceive any fign of Injuftice
' in their Conftitution : He calls them a Na-
' tion of Philofophers, and takes notice that
' the Neighbouring States and Colonies of
' Greece look'd on the City of Sparta as a per-
' fect Model of good Manners, and Wife Go-
' vernment. To go on ; the Surveyor finds fault
because I did not affign the reafon of the Spartans Averfion to the Stage. To this I muft anfwer, I had no mind to tire the Reader with
unneceffary Talk. Who would imagine, but
that fo Wife a Government as the Spartans,
had a good Reafon for their diflike? However he muft garnifh his Margin, and have
the Reafon out, tho it makes againft him.
Here 'tis then : The Lacedemonians allowed
neither Tragedy nor Comedy, that they might not
hear any thing contradictory to their Laws. No :
They had no Palate for the Rapes and Adulteries, and Buffoning Liberties of the Stage.
They would not fuffer the Sobriety of their
Difcipline, and the Gravity of their Conftitution, to be affronted fo much as in jeft.
Yes, the Surveyor grants they were afraid the
Luxury of the Drama, as 'twas practifed at A-
thens, might foften their Youth, and enervate
their Minds : And now had not I great reafon to be afraid of inferting the Citation at
length ? But the Lacedemonians were only concern'd

Marginalia (left column):

Plat.in Lycurg.
Lacon. Inftitut.

Survey, p. 65.

Ut neque joco-
neque ferio eos
qui Legibus
contradicerent
audirent.Lacon.
Inftit.
Survey, p. 65.

Survey, p. 67,
68.

cern'd to preserve the Martial Spirit of their People. Survey, p. 67.
How does that appear? Were the *Lacedemo-nians* only for one good Quality? Had they no concern for the Vertues of Peace, and the Securities of good Correspondence among themselves? That's strange! *Plutarch* calls them a *Nation* of *Philosophers*, and makes them strict Observers of Regularity in general. But for the *Surveyor's* sake, let us suppose them *Ambitious only of Military Glory:* Even this Ibid. Point could not be gained without Sobriety of Manners. For, if we observe, we shall find the *Persians*, *Greeks*, and *Romans*, &c. were always best Soldiers, when they were best Men. Indeed they held their Empire, as it were of Virtue and Moral Philosophy. For when they came to Debauch; they grew quickly good for nothing; and dwindled by degrees from Cowardise to Servitude. Insignificancy, to speak softly, is the Natural Consequence of Lewdness. Dissolution destroys both the Will and the Power to be Serviceable. It makes Men impatient of Discipline, Quarrelsom and Mutinous, and unable to bear the Fatigues of War. A Lewd Soldier often fails in point of Corporal Force, is deserted even by his Limbs, and has no Constitution to be Brave, tho never so willing: I mean as to Campaigning, and a Course of War. Thus when the *Stage* is suffered to Debauch a Nation, and bring Vice into Credit,

dit, People will be in danger of having more Confidence than Courage. This is the way to ſoften a *Martial Spirit*, and deſtroy the Principles of Honour. And thus *Military Glory*, and *Civil* Vertue, and every thing elſe that's worth the owning, muſt take their Leave in a ſhort time. This Conſequence was Wiſely foreſeen by the *Lacedemonians*, and guarded againſt accordingly.

The *Surveyor* rallies once more, and tells us, That *Plutarch* ſays indeed, *that the* Spartans *did not admit Comedy nor Tragedy, but ſays not a ſyllable of Forms, and Regulations.* This is wonderful Civil ! If he grows thus good Natured, I muſt Diſpute with him no longer. I beſeech him, What does he think I argued againſt in the *View*, was it not againſt the Liberties of Tragedy and Comedy ? If he fancies I wrote againſt *Punchianello*, or the *Water-works*, he is much miſtaken. If the *Lacedemonians* refuſed to admit Tragedy, or Comedy upon any Condition, they refuſed to admit them under any Form. To go farther with him, His old Starting Hole is ſtopt, for he can't ſo much as pretend, that the *Mimi* would paſs the Teſt, where the *Drama* was thus diſcouraged. But I am almoſt to blame for taking notice of theſe Objections.

We muſt now take a Turn in *Italy*. From hence I brought a famous Inſtance, how ſeverely the *Roman* Government treated the

Survey, p. 66.

Stage

Stage under all its Latitude and Diſtinctions.
The Authority is no leſs than *Tully*'s, in his
Tract de Republica, cited by St. *Auguſtine* with
Approbation. * To this Teſtimony the *Sur-*
veyor returns a ſurprizing Anſwer. *Since* Tully
does not appear in his own Perſon, we ſhall not
(ſays he) *ſpend any time or Ammunition upon*
him *. Well! Tho his Reſolution is right,
his Reaſon is wrong. For, What tho *Tully*'s
Books *De Republica,* are loſt, they were extant in the time of St. *Auguſtine ?* Is this Father's Credit ſo low, that he can't be truſted
for a Citation ? This Treatiſe of *Tully* was too
well known at that time a day to be counter-
feited ; ſo that if St. *Auguſtine* was unfair in
the Citation, he wanted both common Honeſty, and common Sence. And after all, I
can't perceive that *Tully* has here depoſed
more againſt the *Play-houſe,* than *Livy* did
after him, who comes next to be Examined.
This Author, to make *ſhort* work of the Quotation, informs us, That the *Common Players*
were expelled their Tribe, and refuſed to ſerve in
Arms. Here the *Surveyor* makes a miſerable
Pother ; Reaſons backwards and forwards,
and makes Might and Main for the old Cover
of the *Pantomimes :* And thus by his running
upon the *File ,* and Doubling, we may perceive he is almoſt ſpent. In anſwer to what
he offers, I ſhall firſt take notice of his Con-
ceſſions : He grants, in the firſt place, that
the

* *Romani, ſicut*
apud Ciceronem
idem Scipio lo-
quitur, cum ar-
tem Ludicram
Scenamque
totam probro
ducerent, genus
id hominum
non modo honore
civium reliquo-
rum carere, ſed
etiam tribu
moveri nota-
tione Cenſoriæ
voluerunt.
St. Auguſt de
Civ. Dei Lib.
2. *cap.* 13.
View, p. 240.
* *Survey,* p. 69.

Liv. Dec. 1.
L. 7.
View, p. 241.

the *Romans* went on the same Grounds with the *Lacedæmonians* in discouraging the *Stage.*

Surv. p.70,71. They were afraid their *Military Virtue* might suffer by it: Now of this Supposition I have made my Advantage already.

Surv.p.71,74.
Ibid. *Secondly,* He affirms, That *the Practice of the Stage among the* Romans *fell into the hands of Slaves :* From whence one would imagine 'twas pretty plain that the *Romans* thought this Business was too coarse for Persons of higher Condition. Indeed his Reason for this Custom is very pleasant: He says *this* Ibid. *Profession was thrown up to the Slaves, upon the account of its being a polite Exercise, and too refin'd a Diversion for the rest of the* Roman *Youth.* Now I would gladly know how it comes about, that Slaves are so much better bred than their Masters, and *Mob* than Persons of Quality? Upon the *Surveyor's* State of the Chronology, this was extreamly unlikely: For if this hapned before the Settlement of Surv. p.73. the *Drama*, the time lies against him ; for then the *Romans* had not conquer'd the Polite Countries, nor made any Inroads upon *Asia* or *Greece.* But let *Acting* be as Polite as the *Surveyor* pleases, 'tis plain the *Romans* P. 74. look'd upon it as unreputable, otherwise they would never have left it *wholly in the hands of Slaves and Mercenary Foreigners.* These Concessions one would think were

frank

frank enough ; but we shall have more of his
Liberality by and by ; and in the mean
time I shall consider his Evasions.

In the first place he endeavours to avoid *Surv. p.72,76.*
the Blow, by fencing with the Distinction
between the *Ludi Scenici* and the *Drama:* But
this is meer Supposition and chimerical Fancy,
and directly overthrown by a Quotation of *Surv. p.122.*
his own from St. *Augustine*. *Et hæc sunt Sce-*
nicorum tolerabiliora ludorum, *Comædiæ scilicet* *De Civ. Dei,*
& Tragediæ, &c. The *Surveyor* should take *Lib. 2.*
care to keep his Margin a little in Order ; a
bad *Memory*, and a bad *Cause*, do very ill
together.

Secondly, He argues, That *this Mark of In-*
famy set upon the Histriones, can't properly stick *Surv. p. 73.*
upon the Actors of Tragedy and Comedy as such,
that Law having been made long before the Drama
was brought to Rome. First, with his Favour,
this Mark of Disadvantage must evidently
stick upon the *Actors* of Tragedy, *&c.* and
that by his own Argument: for they, and *Surv. p. 76.*
only they, as himself informs us, were call'd
Histriones. He is now got off the Pin of De-
monstration, and falls down to *Conjectures,*
and argues like any *Almanack:* He fansies *Surv. p. 74.*
therefore the *Mime's and Pantomime's were aim'd*
at in this Law. To this I answer, That having prov'd the Business of the *Mime's, &c. v.d. supra.*
to be originally part of the *Drama*, by consequence if the *Mime's* were struck at by *this*
Law,

Law, the *Drama* will be concern'd in the Correction : For the *Mime's* being, as *Suetonius* tells us, originally part of Comedy, and Comedy, as *Scaliger* obſerves, being prior to the *Mime's*, this Law being an early Proviſion, as the *Surveyor* confeſſes, could not be made before the *Mime's* and the *Drama* were parted; from whence it will follow, that the *Drama* muſt be affected with the *Cenſure*.

Scal. Poet, Lib. 1. c. 10.

And as this Law was an early, ſo 'twas a laſting Check upon the *Stage*, being in force when *Livy* wrote, as appears by the Words of the Citation : * And here the Hiſtorian ſpeaks in comprehenſive Phraſe, and excepting the *Fabulæ Atellanæ*, takes in the *Play-houſe*, with all its Appurtenances; as appears not only from the Term *Hiſtriones*, but from the other expreſſion of *Ars Ludicra*, which, by the Authority of the *Civil Law*, quoted by the *Surveyor*, includes all the Denominations and Diſtinctions of the *Stage*.

Eò inſtitutum manet, &c.

Ab Hiſtrionibus pollui. Expertes artis Ludicræ. Surv. p. 77.

And now having evidently proved the *Dramatick Actors* under the Diſcouragement of the *Roman Conſtitution*, we need not ſtand to the Courteſie of his Suppoſition, for to that, after a little ſtruggling, he is willing to come. Nay, at laſt he yields up the Suppoſition for matter of Fact, and cites a *Prætorian* Edict, hinted by the *View*, in proof of it; and be-

cauſe

cause I suppose he wont quarrel at his own
Translation, it shall serve instead of the Latin:
Whoever (as the Edict runs) *appears on the
Stage to Speak or Act , is declar'd Infamous.*
Here the *Surveyor* can't deny but *Comedians* Surv. p. 77, 78.
and *Tragedians* are included. But then he
alledges, That *their Profession was not branded* Ibid. p. 80.
*on the score of Immorality, but because they ex-
ercis'd it for Hire.* This being his last Refuge, I shall endeavour to drive him out
on't, and prove in contradiction to his Af-
sertion, That the *Play-house* was censur'd by
the *Romans* upon the Charge of *Immorality*,
and because of the Scandal of their Performances; and that 'twas the *Nature of their
Profession,* and not the *Mercenary Condition of* Surv. p. 80.
exercising it, which drew the Censure upon them.

First then, We may learn from *Tully*, as *Artem Ludi-*
St. *Augustine* cites him, that the *Romans cram scenamque
look'd* upon the Business of *Players* as igno- totam probro du-
minious in all the Parts of it; and as *Go-* cer.nt, De Civ.
thofred* expresses it , 'twas counted *turpe mu-* Dei. Lib. 2. c.
nus,* a *scandalous Profession.* This Mark of 13.
View, p. 241.
Disadvantage we see comes full upon the
Function; there's no Conditions of Favour
or Exceptions for Acting *gratis.* This State
of Ignominy was not the Punishment of
meer *Hire:* The *Romans* were not expell'd
their Tribe , and thrown out of Common
Privilege only for taking Money for their
Labour: No; they Fought for Pay, and
Pleaded for Fees, and Traded for Gain too,
without any such Disadvantage to their
E   Con-

Condition. Why then fhould Mettals tranf-
mute backwards in the *Play-houfe*, and Money look fo dull and fcandalous in the *Actors*
Pockets? Why fhould the Confideration of
Gain blaft their Character, forfeit their
Right, and extinguifh the Privileges they
were born to? Why, I fay, fhould the *Roman Players* have fuch ill luck with their Money more than other People, unlefs becaufe
they were thought not to come handfomly
by it? This extraordinary Ufage plainly af-
fects the Matter, and proves the Myftery
unreputable: And therefore the latter *Law*
cited by the *Surveyor*, does nothing of his Bufinefs. However, it fhall be tranfcrib'd.

*Thofe that appear upon the Stage for Gain,
are Infamous,* fays *Pegafus* and *Nerva* the Son.
Now by what I have already difcourr'd, 'tis
plain that thefe Words were defign'd to check
the Avarice of the *Romans*, and to keep them
from enriching themfelves by a Libertine
Profeffion ; and that if they were refolv'd
to live upon the Practice, they fhould pay
for't in their Character and Credit. In fhort,
the Intention of this Law was to hinder
them from dangerous Bufinefs, and to make
them more in love with Probity than Money.

Secondly, That the *Play-houfe* at *Rome* was
cenfur'd for *Immorality*, may be farther un-
deniably prov'd from *Valerius Maximus*, who
mentioning the Rife of *Plays* much after the
fame manner with *Livy*, gives the Reafon
why the *Actors* of the *Fabulæ Attellanæ* had
better

better Quarter than the rest of the *Players :*
' And this was, because this Diversion was
' clean and inoffensive, and made agreeable
' to the Sobriety of the *Roman* Discipline.
'Twas form'd, as *Casaubon* observes, upon the
Modesty of the Old Satyr, and was much
more Merry than Mad. ' This Staunchness,
' as *Maximus* goes on, screen'd the *Actors* from
' Disgrace, and purchas'd their Patent of
' Indemnity : So that they were neither (like
' the rest of the *Stage*) expell'd their Tribe,
' nor refus'd to serve in the Field.

*Quod genus de-
lectationis Ita-
lica severitate
temperatum,
ideoque vacu-
um nota est :
nam neque tri-
bu movetur,
neque a mili-
taribus stipen-
diis repellitur,
Valer. Max.
Lib. 2. c. 4.
Casaub. in Loc.*

    The *Surveyor* proceeds to acquaint us, That
Tully, tho' *a Man of great Vanity and Caution,
contracted an intimate Friendship with* Roscius
an Actor, therefore the Business of the Stage
was not unreputable. What *Tully's* Opinion
was of the *Stage,* has been sufficiently shewn
already : As to this Objection, 'tis so fully
obviated in the *View,* &c. by *Tully* himself,
that I can't imagine why the *Surveyor* mention'd it, unless to fill up the *Page.* But
Tully made an Acquaintance with *Roscius :*
Most certainly, *Roscius* was considerable in
his way, and it seems one of the most Moral
in his Profession : And besides, 'tis likely *Tully*
might learn something of Gesture and Pro-
nunciation of him. In short, *Tully* lik'd the
Man, but not his Business. For all that, he
defended his Cause. That's true ; he defended
him in an Action of Debt : But what's that
to his Profession ? Can't a Lawyer plead for
his Client, without justifying his Practise,

Surv. p. 82.

View, p. 274,
275.

View, ibid.
Surv. p. 82.

and

and anfwering for his Trade ? But I'm afraid
I have confider'd this fort of Reafoning too
much, and therefore fhall proceed.

Surv. p. 80. The *Surveyor* urges, That *Scipio Africanus* and
Lalius were publickly fufpected to have affifted Terence *in the Compofition of his Plays.* Sufpect-
ed! Then it feems 'twas no very creditable
Bufinefs. This is an odd way of Arguing,
if pofitive Evidence from unexceptionable
Hiftory and *Law,* may be fet afide by remote
Conjectures, which would fignifie nothing,
if prov'd; I fay, if the beft Evidence may
be thus over-rul'd, we muft never prove
Ufefulnefs of
the Stage, p.
92. any thing. This Objection was made by
Mr. *Dennis*, and is fufficiently anfwer'd in
my *Defence*, by the Counter-evidence of
Defence, &c.
p. 85, 86. *Scipio Nafica* and *Horace.* But let us fuppofe,
if you pleafe, which the Inftance is far from
proving, That *Africanus* and *Lalius* believ'd
the Stage not difcourag'd on the fcore of
Immorality; the Confequence will only be
this, That thefe two Perfons were of one
Opinion, and the Government of another;
and thus their Authority is deftroy'd by running counter to the *Law.* This Anfwer will
affect his Objections from the Two *Cæfars*
and *Seneca*; which being weaker than the
reft, I fhall confider them no farther.

Ufefulnefs of
the Stage, p.
99. My Inftance in the *Theodofian Code*, Mr. *Dennis* gives up for an *unreafonable Cuftom*; but
the *Surveyor*, who loves neither Yielding nor
Proving, encounters the Authority with a
Banter. He finds fault indeed with the
Tran-

Tranſlation; but diſproves it in no particular: But fails in his own *Verſion* by his own Rule; for he renders *Hiſtrio* by *Droll-Actor*, whereas he has already told us, that this *Word* is peculiar to the top Function of the Stage, *Surv. p. 76.* and ſignifies the *Players* in their beſt Capacity. Farther, by his citing the Law at length, it appears, that *Hiſtrio*, or an *Actor* in the *Drama*, has as little a Character as a *Pantomime :* Nay, the Language falls rather harder upon the firſt ; for the *Pantomime* does not ſuffer ſo much in the *Addition*, nor *Pantomimum* has that Epithe of Diſadvantage which de-*veſte humili,* ſcribes the other. And thus by his Criti-*aut vilem offe-rat Hiſtrionem,* ciſms and Exactneſs, he has made the Tran-*&c.* ſlation worſe, and the Caſe worſe.

I have now gone through his Charge againſt the Teſtimonies in the laſt Chapter of the *View*, &c. and I hope fully ſhewn that my Authors have been fairly tranſlated and rightly applied. The Objections againſt the Pagan part of the Authorities, were moſt of them made by Mr. *Dennis* before the *Surveyor :* The Anſwers to the one therefore will hold againſt the other. But Mr. *Den-*Uſefulneſs of *nis* has one Exception about St. *Auguſtine* par-*the Stage, p.* ticular to himſelf ; 'tis this: He ſays St. *Au-*90. *guſtine*, as *I have cited him*, * *has done* Cicero *a* * *Nonne Cicero* great deal of wrong, in the Character of *Roſcius.* *eorum cum Roſ-cium quædam* In the firſt place, my Citation of St. *Auguſtine* *laudaret Hi-* is right to a tittle ; and therefore I can have *ſtrionem ; ita* nothing to anſwer for. And that St. *Auguſtine* *p ritum dixit ut ſolus eſſet*

E 3 was

dignus qui in scenam debere intrare: ita virum bonum ut solus esset dignus qui eo non aberet accedere quid aliud apertissime ostendens nisi illam scenam esse tam turpem, ut tanto minus ibi esse homo debeat, quanto magis fuerit vir bonus. Aug. de Consensu Evangelist, Lib. 1. View, &c. p. 274.

was the least to blame, we have no just Reason to suspect. For, first, we are to observe, that *Tully's* Oration, *Pro Roscio*, cited by Mr. *Dennis*, is a great part of it lost, we have neither beginning nor end of it. But in St. *Augustine's* time *Tully's* Works were entire. Now because a Passage is not in part of an Argument, to conclude it was not there at all, is an odd way of reasoning. And if 'twas not in this Oration, there was room enough for it in the rest of *Tully's* Works, which are now lost.

Secondly, The Words and Sence of this Quotation, and that cited by Mr. *Dennis*, are so very different, that 'tis next to impossible, that St. *Augustine*, if he quoted from Memory, should mistake the one for the other: And yet he quotes it roundly, and Reasons positively upon it. From whence (says this Father) *Tully was most clearly of Opinion, that the better a Man was, the less fit he was to make a Player*. And can we imagine a Person of S. *Augustin's* Character, could mistake so mark'd and memorable a Sentence? He that was so well acquainted with the Heathen Learning, and particularly with *Tully*, having publickly taught Rhetorick in his younger time? To change the Words of an Author to so strange a Degree, to so very foreign a signification, could be nothing but Design. Now can we imagine that St. *Augustine's* Conscience could digest such a Practice as this? Would he who had wrote a whole Books against Falshood and Lying, be guilty

in

of fo notorious an Inftance himfelf? What, in an Author fo well known as *Tully*, in a Sentence fo very remarkable, and in a Treatife written for the Satisfaction of the Heathens? For now we are to obferve, that St. *Auguftine* was encountring fome Pagan Objections about the Gofpels, and proving the Confiftency of the *Evangelifts* with each other. Befides, there was no neceffity for fo wretched and ridiculous an Expedient: The Controverfie did not languifh for this Citation; for as pertinent as it was, St. *Auguftine* could eafily have gone on without it. But poffibly the *Reader* may think I have taken too much notice of a Calumny fo much without colour: To return therefore to the *Surveyor*.

And here once for all, I can't but wonder at his Captioufnefs and Noife againft the Method of my Quotations: *The Authors*, fays he, *were not cited at length, and in their own Language, which it feems could be nothing but Defign.* That my Meaning was fair, I have made good already; and that my Method was defenfible, is no lefs plain, for I always took care to cite *Book, Chapter*, or *Page*, and fometimes *Edition* too. Now how could Impofition and foul Play lie hid under fuch a Punctuality? When this was done, what need was there of ftuffing the *Margin* with Greek and Latin? Why fhould I give my felf a needlefs Fatigue, and trouble the *Englifh Reader* with a foreign Language to no purpofe? All unneceffary Quoting is either

Pedan-

Pedantry or Oftentation. The *Surveyor* has neither Reafon nor Cuftom for his Demands. What then would the Man be at? I hope he did not expect I fhould get a *Certificate*, or make *Affidavit* in proof of my Authorities? 'Tis true, his making a fquabble about the Teftimonies has now fomewhat alter'd the Cafe; Infomuch that I am fometimes forced to bring him to the Teft of the Original, to difcover his Honefty.

And now having fet the Teftimonies right, the reft of the *Surveyor's* Book will go off apace.

The *Surveyor* Complains of my Cenfuring the *Mufick and Geftures of the Playhoufe only upon Report, having never heard of one, nor feen t'other.* As to the Playhoufe Mufick, he has given me no occafion to refume that Argument, neither did I meddle with their Dancing. But here he runs too faft. I only told him, I was no Frequenter of the *Playhoufe.* I muft tell him, I have been there, tho: not always for Diverfion. I am not fo much a Stranger to that place, as not to have feen the Behaviour of their Women bold, and the Geftures lewd fometimes, witnefs the *Hoftefs in Bartholomew Fair!* His appeal to the Ladies in this Cafe is ftrangely out of the way. He has reproach'd them too much in the *Dedication,* either to expect their Favour, or depend on their Decifion. The Outrage is very grofs and comprehenfive, as will appear at the firft fight. *Women,* fays the

Surveyor, p 99.

View, p. 278.

the *Surveyor* to the Earl of *Dorset*, and weak *Epist. Ded.*
Men, *whose Fears are stronger than their Judg-*
ments, will be awed into a Perswasion before they
are convinced of the Truth of it. For *such People,*
in most Cases, measure the certainty of Asserti-
ons by the Confidence of him that pronounces them.
Here's a Flourish for ye upon the whole *Sex !*
Here's Decency of Application, and Strains
of Breeding and Conduct ! And does the
Surveyor call in the Ladies to Vouch for him
after this Usage ? After he has disabled their
Character, and thrown them out of Sence
and Capacity ? His Modesty and Judgment,
I perceive, are much of a size : These Com-
plaints, I suppose, were calculated for *Russia*,
or rather for *Constantinople*, where the Women are said to have no Souls. I asserted in
the *View*, *&c.* with reference to the *English*
Stage, That if *they have any advantage in their*
Instrumental Musick, they lose it in their Vocal :
Their Songs *being often rampantly lewd, and ir-*
religious to a flaming excess : Now the ancients, *View*, p. 280.
as we have seen already, were inoffensive in this
respect. Here the *Surveyor* falls a railing very
liberally, and if his Logick would but answer his Language, there was no enduring
him : But the best on't is, his Reasoning
usually makes amends for his Railing : And
so it happens at present, for at the first open-
ing of the Cause, he does no less than give
it up. He grants the Chorus of the *Ancients*
was harmless enough. But then the Reason he *Survey*, p. 103.
proves it by is somewhat untoward. This
Musick

P. 101.

Mufick, fays he, *confifted of Hymns and Praifes of their Gods, and therefore Lewdnefs would have been impertinent.* On the contrary, the Pagan Idols were lewd, and their Worfhip was lewd, and if the Hymns had been fo too, they had been all of a Piece. Where then was the impropriety ? But then this, as St. *Paul* obferves, was for the moft part *done in fecret :* For Nature was not wholly fubdued by Idolatry. 'Twas therefore the force of Modefty, and the regards of Virtue, which made the Chorus inoffenfive, and not Compliance with Religion, as the *Surveyor* fuggefts. And is not the ancient Stage much better than the Modern upon this account ? For they declin'd Smutt, tho their Religion allow'd it. But thefe are refolv'd to charge through their Creed, and to have it at any purchafe of Infamy and Danger. To return to the *Chorus,* if that was inoffenfive, as the *Surveyor* truly affirms, then the Vocal Stage Mufick of the Ancients was inoffenfive, for they had no Songs but in the *Chorus* ; I Challenge the *Surveyor* to produce one elfewhere in all the Old Tragedy and Comedy extant : And does it not follow from hence, that the old *Drama* was inoffenfive, not only upon the Comparifon, but even without it ? His running off to the grofs Liberties of the *Mimi* is a poor relief : For, *Firft,* By thus retreating from the Subject, he quits the Field, and leaves the *Antient Drama* in poffeffion of the Advantage contefted.

Secondly,

Secondly, In all his Ramble and Aggravation about the *Mimi*, he neither offers to prove his Point by Argument or Testimony: He neither gives any Instance, nor cites any Author; so that the whole of his Cause lies only in Affirmation and Assurance. His saying, That *all who are acquainted with the* Roman *Stage, know his Charge against the Mimi to be true*, is like the rest. I must tell him, he does not know it to be true, and therefore should not object it. Nay, as far as it appears 'tis untrue; for the Lewdness of the *Mimi* consisted more in Gesture, than Expression. I charged the Stage *with encouraging* View, p. 283. *Revenge, and mistaking the Notion of Honour:* This he denies, and would make us believe, that a Vindictive Humour is *almost always made the Mark of a Tyrant or a Villain in Tra-* Survey, p. 108: *gedy.* But by his Instance in *Don Manuel* he mistakes the Point: The Disorders of Princes was not the Dispute in that place: 'Twas private Revenge which was principally aimed at, as appears by the mention of *Duelling.* And is not this Humour incouraged by the *Stage?* Don't their Characters of Figure quarrel in *Comedy*, and Murther in *Tragedy?* Is it not Honourable to do it, and Infamous to refuse it? And thus, by these Maxims, a Man is bound to be Damn'd in Defence of his Honour, and can't be a Christian without being reckon'd a Poltron. To say this, Frensy is countenanced in Life, and that *a Poet is obliged to draw according to Nature is a lamen-*

table

table Plea. At this rate Rapes and Adulteries
must be Acted, and all sort of Blasphemy
repeated, that Nature may be shewn in her
Colours: But this I have answered already.
And therefore his saying, That *there can be
no Breach of Morality, without offending against
the Laws of the Drama*; His saying this, is in
effect, to make the Poets Soveraign Judges of
Good and Evil; To give the Stage a Power
Paramount to Gospel and Law, and to make
Vice the Standart of Virtue. By this Doctrine they may bring all the Stench of the
Stews upon the Board, and Poyson *Cum Pri-
vilegio.* For, what is all this, but a close
Imitation of Life? Now if *any Man dislikes
these Figures, let him do it at his Peril,* says the
*Surveyor, for then he finds fault with Nature,
not with the Poet.* Nay, if *those Pictures be
drawn according to the Life, he might as well
snarl at the Wise Providence which governs the
World, because he meets more ugly Faces then
handsome ones, more Knaves and Fools than Ho-
nest Men, &c.* This is admirable Reasoning!
For, in the first place, to suppose Ugliness so
very common, is a Satyr upon Mankind, and
is remote both from Truth, and Deceney:
But to make *Knavery* the effect of *Providence,*
as this Author does by the drift of his Reasoning, and the force of his Comparison, is
next to Blasphemy. To proceed from his
Supposition to his Inference: Does the *Surveyor* think there's no difference between Natural Defects and Moral Turpitude, and are

ugly

View, p. 35, 383.

Defence, p. 10, 15, &c.

Surv. p. 119.

Ibid.

Ugly Faces as catching as Ugly Practices?
Certainly, no. The Deformities of Behaviour
are much more dangerous than those of Person and Understanding. Lewdness and A-
theism are infectious, but Folly is a disadvantage to none but him that has it. Now,
if we are obliged to guard our Virtue, and
avoid ill Discourse, Why not in the Play-
house, as well as in other places? Unless we'l
say, that the Wit and Figure, and Success of a
Libertine mortifies his Example, and makes him
less dangerous: And then by the same Rule we
may conclude, that the malignity of a Di-
stemper is a good symptom of Health, and
that People are likely to do least mischief,
when they are best prepared for't.

I must now attend the *Surveyor* in his Examination of the *Greek* and *Roman Tragedy*, in
which he pretends the *Ancients* were defective
in the Morality of their *Fable*. And upon *Survey*, p. 126.
the comparison of some few Instances, endeavours to throw the preference upon the
Moderns. In this Enquiry he spends a great
part of his Book, which were it never so
lucky, would be but little to his purpose.
For, to say no more at present, this Justification would reach no farther than Tragedy,
Comedy does not enter the Dispute upon this
Head, and therefore must be left defenceless.
He throws away abundance of Ammunition
upon this *place*, which if he could carry it,
would not be worth the Storming: This will
appear upon the progress of the Contest;

and

and in the mean time I shall endeavour to repel the Attack, and disappoint him in the little Advantage.

In pursuing this Point, the *Surveyor* falls into a mighty Vein of telling *Stories*, which by the length and manner of them, one would fancy were told more for his own Diversion, than the *Readers*. Here we must take him by Tale, and not by Weight; measure his Arguments by the Page; And if a Man could be confuted by the Yard, he might possibly have done my Business.

He begins with the Fable of *Sophocles* his *Oedipus*, and Censures it for *being very deficient in the Moral*. And yet in the next Words he owns *it may serve to put us in mind of the Lubricity of Fortune, and the Instability of Humane Greatness*. Call you this *Moral* very deficient! Does it not hold forth a Lesson of Justice and Moderation to great Men? Does it not teach the proper use of Prosperity, and prepare us for the Turns of Adversity? This *Moral* is so far from being deficient in a Play, that it would make a good Sermon. But the ground of the Quarrel is, this *Moral* is too good for such a Heathen as *Sophocles*, and therefore he must not have it. Not have it! What, tho the Poem uses it expresly as such? that's confessed: For all that the *Surveyor* not only finds fault with Mr. *Dryden*, but wont give *Sophocles* leave to understand the Moral of his own *Fable*. This is very hard. But since he is resolv'd to refine

Survey, p. 131.

Survey, p. 131.

P. 133.

refine upon *Sophocles* and Mr. *Dryden*, let's see what he'l make on't. Now this Gentleman tells us, that the *genuine Moral of the Fable* ought to have been shewn in setting forth *Oedipus*'s ; *Misfortunes*, as a result of his *Impiety, in advancing his own Judgment above that of his Gods ; and thinking by his own Wisdom to reverse the immutable Decrees of Destiny, and upon this account his Vanity deserv'd the heaviest Chastisement.* To this I answer,

First, That if this were the *Moral,* it would not be without Instruction : It might shew the vanity of contesting with Omnipotence, and teach submission to the Decrees of Heaven, that People should conclude the Punishment just by the Hand that sent it, and not repine at the Mysteries of Providence.

But *Secondly,* That this Sence is not *the genuine Moral,* appears by the *Surveyor's* Objection, in which he grants, That Predestination *was not so universal among the Antient Heathens, but many held the contrary.* And if Oedipus *was one of this Number, he grants his Moral falls to the Ground.* Now, that *Oedipus* was no Predestinarian, I think is pretty clear from his Management : For if he believed a Fatality, he must believe his Misfortunes irretrievable, and why then was he so weak as to attempt the preventing it ? Why then did he quit his Fortune and his Friends, throw up the Expectations of a Crown, and run rambling after a known Impossibility ? Such a Piece of Pilgrimage is fitter for a Goose then

Survey, p. 133, 145.

Ibid.

then a Hero, especially one who could look through Mysteries, untie Riddles, and had a reach of Understanding above the rest of Mankind. 'Tis plain therefore, *Oedipus* did not imagine himself under a Necessity of of Murthering his Father. He thought the Oracle pronounced no more then a Conditional Truth ; He took it for a fair warning, but believed the Event might be secur'd by Care, and Caution.

Farther, By this Scheme of Fatality the reason of Punishment is destroyed, and by consequence the *Moral* sinks with it. For, why should *Oedipus* be punished for attempting to *reverse Destiny*, when all his Actions were pre-ordain'd, and he had not so much as his own Will in his power ? Where there is no Choice, there can be no Fault : Alass! Upon this Supposition his *Vanity* was unavoidable, and he could no more help the contesting with Fate, than he could over-rule it. For as the *Surveyor* has it from *Seneca*,

Quicquid patimur mortale genus,
Quicquid facimus venit ab alto.

To make *Oedipus* smart for questioning the Oracle in this Case, is against all Reason and Justice : And the Poet might as well have brought him to Execution, because he could not fly. And thus we see the Poet will shift much better by himself than with the *Surveyor's* Assistance. The *Moral* of the rest of
Sophocles's

Sophocles's Plays is either good, or not bad, by Survey. p, 150, to 165. his own Confession, and therefore that Dispute is at an end : 'Tis true he excepts a little against *Hyllus's* Expostulation with the Gods. Soph. Trachin. But this Objection was started, and consider'd in the *View, &c.* View, p. 91.

Orestes's killing his Mother, tho not Censur'd by the *Surveyor*, lies harder upon *Sophocles* than the other. But when we consider, that he was put upon this Practice by the *Oracle*, to revenge his Father's Murther, Sophoc. Electr. Act 1. and the Abuse of his Bed ; This Consideration, I say, upon the Heathen Theology, seems to excuse the Fact.

We are now to proceed to *Euripides*, who is blam'd by the *Surveyor* for not contriving Survey, p. 164, 178. his Fable to the Advantage of his *Moral*. To this it may be return'd, That his Instances of Mismanagement in this Poet are but few : And even all of those few * won't hold ; * Ibid. and where they do, the Plays are defensible upon another Head.

And because he makes *Orestes*, and the other produced by him, a Sample of the rest, it may not be amiss to shew the *Reader* in a Word or two, how unfairly *Euripides* is represented by the *Surveyor*.

To begin, *Hecuba* his first Play, has a *Moral* sufficiently instructive. For, here *Polydorus* comes from the other World to discover Treachery and Murther. And *Polymnestor*, King of *Thrace*, being the guilty Person, is

punished

punish'd with the loss of his Eyes : This Piece of Revenge is executed by *Hecuba*, Mother to the Murther'd Person, and being question'd for the Fact, she is acquitted by *Agamemnon* ; as indeed she well might, having done nothing unjustifiable by the Principles of Paganism.

The *Phæniſſæ* is full of *Moral* Sentences, and as to the *Fable*, the Misfortune of *Laius* and his Posterity is declared to proceed from his disobedience to the Oracle : which holds forth this Lesson, That 'tis dangerous to go counter to the Instructions of Heaven ; and that our Duty should always over-rule our Desires.

Eurip. Phæniſſ. p. 112. Ed. Cantabr.

Hippolitus Coronatus is taxed by the *Surveyor* with a defective *Moral*, because an inoffensive young Prince of that Name miscarries in't. But this *Fable*, if we look farther, has a great deal of good meaning in't. For *Hippolitus* is visited in his Misfortunes by a Goddess who clears his Innocence, undertakes his Quarrel, and promises to immortalize his Memory.

Hippol. p. 262, &c.

The *Surveyor* grants *Alcestis* a Moral Play, and the same may be said of *Andromache* : For here *Hermione*, who injur'd the Royal Captive *Andromache*, grows almost distracted with her guilt, and is hardly prevented from dispatching her self.

Androm. p. 319, 320. Androm. p. 329, 330.

Menelaus likewise designing to Murther *Andromache* and her Son *Moloſſus*, is disappointed in his Barbarity by *Peleus*, who

comes

comes in the nick of time to the rescue of
the Innocent. And at the end of the *Play*,
Andromache is left in possession of the Country, Married to *Helenus*, *Hector*'s Brother,
and the Crown settled upon her Son *Molos-
sus*: And to enrich the *Moral* farther, the
Generous and Compassionate *Peleus* is Deifyed
by *Thetis*, and transported to the Fortunate *Androm. p.*
Islands. *329, 330.*

The Moral of the *Supplices* is not amiss.
The Case stood thus. *Creon* King of *Thebes*
refusing Burial to the Chiefs slain before that
Town, *Adrastus*; the only surviving Confe-
derate, applies to *Theseus* King of *Athens*, for
Assistance, desiring to be put into a Condition to take care of the Funerals of his
Friends. For to have these Solemnities un-
perform'd, was a sad misfortune among the
Heathens, who believed the Ghosts of the
Deceased had no rest, till their Bodies were
burnt, and their Bones buried, according to
that of *Virgil*.

Nec ripas datur horrendas & rauca fluenta
Transportare, prius quam sedibus ossa quierunt.

The Request being thus reasonable, *The-
seus* complies with it, and having demanded
Justice of *Creon* by an Embassy to no purpose,
he goes against him in Person, defeats his
Forces in the Field, and recovers the dead
Bodies of the *Generals*.

This Expedition was a generous Instance
of Humanity to the Dead, and Living, and
there-

therefore the Poet rewards him with fuccefs. The Fable likewife teaches us, That the Dead are not to be infulted, nor the Vanquifhed refufed in their reafonable Demands.

To proceed. His *Iphigenia in Aulide* has a turn of Virtue in the Contrivance. For here *Agamemnon* refigns in a very tender Point to the Orders of the Gods, and was willing to Sacrifice his Daughter to the Succefs of the Expedition : To let us underftand, that Piety ought to prevail againft Natural Affection, and private Regards give way to publick Intereft. And as for Innocent *Iphigenia*, fhe is refcued from the Slaughter by a Miracle, and preferr'd to be a Prieftefs to *Diana*.

Iphigenia in *Tauris* continues the Story of the Tragedy laft mentioned. Here *Pylades* and *Oreftes* make an Adventure together, and by the Direction of the Oracle arrive at *Tauri* to bring off the Statue of *Diana*. But being feiz'd before they could embark, they were condemn'd to be Sacrificed according to the Cuftom of the Country. *Iphigenia*, the Prieftefs of *Diana*, underftanding the Prifoners to be *Greeks*, refolved to fave one of them, and difpatch him with a Letter to *Argos*. Upon this there follows a noble Conteft between *Pylades* and *Oreftes*, who offer'd to die for each other. But before *Oreftes*, who got the better of his Friend, came to fuffer, he is by good Fortune difcover'd, and own'd by his Sifter *Iphigenia* ; who thereupon con-

contrives their Escape, and goes away with
them. From whence we may learn how un-
expectedly Providence steps in to the Assistance of Friendship and Generosity : And
that he who goes on the Messages of Heaven,
has his Security in his Commission.

The next is the Tragedy of *Rhesus*, which
whether it belongs to *Euripides* or not, is un-
certain. This Prince is surpriz'd in the night
by the Enemy and slain, and seems to miscarry for want of Discipline and Care in the
Army. He may be likewise punish'd for his
Presumption, and for confiding too much in
himself.

In the *Troades Minerva* resolves to punish
the *Greeks* for using their Victory ill, and
particularly for outraging her Priestess *Cas-
sandra*. The rest of the *Play* is little more
than a Relation of the Misfortunes, and
Burning of *Troy* ; so that the *Moral*, as far
as it reaches, is not unserviceable.

The *Bacchæ* is a very Religious *Fable* ; The
Chorus in the 3d Act are admirably Sententious against Atheism and Impiety. And
at last the Misfortunes of *Pentheus* and *Agave*
are declar'd to have happen'd for the Con- Baccha, p.
tempt of the Deity.
206.

The *Moral* of the *Cyclops* gives much the Cyclops, p
same warning with the former ; *Polyphemus* 218, & als &
being here punish'd for his Atheistical Rants,
and inhospitable Temper.

In

In the next Play *Euriftheus* fmarts for perfecuting the *Heraclidæ*. Thefe injur'd Perfons are affifted by the *Athenians*, defeat the Ufurper, and recover their Right. To fay no more, this *Play* threatens Pride with Divine Vengeance, and pleads ftrongly for Juftice and Religion.

The Tragedy of *Helena* gives Countenance to Probity : For, by the Structure of the *Fable*, *Helena* is a Lady of Virtue, undebauch'd by *Paris*, and never at *Troy :* She is detain'd Prifoner in *Egypt*, and proves conftant to her Husband *Menelaus*, tho courted by *Theoclymenus* King of that Country. In fhort, fhe conceals *Menelaus* upon his arrival, makes the King believe he was Wreck'd, and defiring leave to folemnize his Funeral on the Shoar, gets an opportunity to efcape the Tyrant, and fet fail. *Theoclymenus* finding himfelf betray'd, and fufpecting his Sifter *Theonoe* in the Plot, refolves to Murther her ; but is perfwaded to defift, and brought to Temper by the *Machine* of *Caftor* and *Pollux*. Here the *Moral* lies upon the furface, is apparently virtuous, and therefore I fhall fay no more about it.

To conclude, *Euripides*'s *Electra* ftands upon the fame foot of Excufe with that of *Sophocles*, and therefore I fhall pafs it over.

From this fhort Survey the Reader may perceive, that much the major part of *Euripides*'s *Plays* are unexceptionable in their *Moral* ; And that Poetick Juftice was generally the

the Poet's Care: Which appears farther by his Apology for his *Ixion*. For, some of the Audience censuring the Conduct of this *Play*, for suffering *Ixion* to flourish, and thrive upon this Wickedness; The Poet desires them to have Patience, for, says he, I broke him upon the *Wheel* at last, and then he paid for all. *Vit. Eurip. Ed. Cantabr.*

The *Surveyor* therefore is much mistaken in making the *Ancients* so negligent in their *Fable:* As if a good *Moral* from them was rather the effect of Casualty than Choice. There are four Tragedies of *Euripides* still unmention'd; that is, his *Orestes*, *Medea*, *Hercules Furens*, and *Ion:* Here I confess the Byass of the Fable is not so well contriv'd, as in the rest. *Survey, p. 194.*

But then he may be in a great measure excused upon these Two following Considerations:

First, Because *Euripides* takes care to correct the Malignity of his Fable by Moral Sentences, and Philosophical Advice, of which, as the *Surveyor* confesses, he is very liberal. Yes: *The Ancients*, says he, *deliver'd their Instructions in Wise Sayings scatter'd in the Dialogue, or at the Close;* Now these *Sentences* were possibly more intelligible to a Common Understanding, than the Mystery of *Plots*, and the Revolution of *Fables:* And therefore when the rest of the *Play* was not stuffed with Lewdness, might govern in the Minds of an Audience, and make a signifi- *Survey, p. 164.* *p. 191.*

cant

cant Impreſſion : But, *Secondly*, That which
goes fartheſt in the Juſtification of *Euripides*
is, that the Diſpoſition of the *Fable* was ſel-
dom in his power : The Subject was generally Hiſtory, or received Tradition ; from
which 'twas unſafe to vary. For, to croſs
upon common Belief, and give Matter of
Fact the Lye, was the way to ſpoil the Pro-
bability and Reliſh of the Poem. The Antients therefore, as the *Surveyor* remarks from
Ariſtotle, being forc'd to take the *Fable* as
they found it, the fault lay in the Hiſtory,
which made the Poet more excuſable.

Surv. p. 187, 188.

And this may ſerve to ſhew, that *Euripides* is much better complexion'd than the
Surveyor was pleas'd to draw him. He is
miſtaken likewiſe in affirming, That *Euripides
does not touch the Paſſions like* Sophocles : For,
no leſs a Judge than *Quintilian* gives him the
preference : *He had*, ſays he, *an admirable
ſtroak at the Pathos in general ; And for raiſing
Compaſſion, was clearly ſuperior to* Sophocles.
And if *Quintilian*'s Authority ſtood in need
of being confirm'd, the Poet *Hippolitus Coronatus*, to ſay nothing farther, might vouch
for him.

Survey. p. 164.

In affectibus vero cum omni-bus mirus, tum in iis, qui miſe-ratione con-ſtant, facile praecipuus. Quintil. Inſtit. Lib. 10. cap. 1.

From *Euripides* the *Surveyor* goes backward
to *Æſchylus*, but this *Poet* will quickly be diſ-
engag'd, for the whole Attack is made only
upon a Sentence or two in his *Promotheus
Vinctus*. But here he is out again in his Impeachment, and miſrepreſents the Reaſon of
Promotheus's Puniſhment. For 'twas not meer
good

Survey, p. 180.

good Nature that made *Promotheus* miscarry. 'Twas becauſe he made bold with *Jupiter's* Prerogative, broke into his Adminiſtration, and diſpos'd of his Bounty againſt his Will.

> ————Τοῖας δ᾽ τις
> Ἁ Καρπίας ὀτὲ Δεῖ Θεοῖς δῦναι δίκην
> Ὡς ἂν διδαχθῆ ἢ Διὸς τυραννίδα
> Στέρξειν————

Prom. Vinct. p. 6, 8, *Ed. Stanl.*

And in the next Page:

> Θεὸς Θεῶν γὰρ ἐχ ὑποπλήσσων χόλον,
> Βροτοῖσι τιμὰς ὤπασας πέρα δίκης.

Promotheus pretended it ſeems to under-ſtand what was fit for the World better than *Jupiter*, and to love Mankind more than he that made them. Now to do this, is Arro-gance, and Imputation with a Witneſs. Be-ſides, as appears in the latter part of the Play, he ſcorn'd a releaſe from his Torments, menaced his pretended Supream, and rattled his Chains againſt his Judge. *View*, p. 87.

But 'tis high time for the *Surveyor* to quit the Coaſt of *Greece*, having met with no Prize after all his Cruiſing. He is now ſail-ing homewards, and trying to mend his Voyage, by touching at *Rome*. And, to conclude the Allegory, *Seneca* is the Man, to make his Fortunes.

And

And here he would perfwade the *Reader*,
Survey. p. 183. that I *took all* Seneca's *Plays for the Work of
one Man.* His Reafon is, I fuppofe, becaufe
I call'd them *Seneca's Tragedies:* Becaufe I did
not diftinguifh between the *Plays* written by
Marcus, and thofe by *Lucius Annæus Seneca* ;
and run out into Pedantry and Foreign Ob-
fervation. But enough of this.

The *Surveyor* remarks, that all *Seneca's Tra-*
P. 182. *gedies are of Greek Extraction :* (for the *Octa-
via* is not worth the naming.) They are fo.
And fo much the better, for then, where
they need it, what I have offer'd for the
Greeks, may ferve for their Apology. Then
the Plan of the *Fable* takes it's refuge in *Hiftory* ; and comes down with Excufe to the
Poet. Befides, the *Surveyor* takes notice, that
Survey. p. 189. *Seneca* refines upon the Juftice of *Euripides*
in his *Hippolytus,* and mends his *Moral.* Why,
this is juft as one would wifh. But then the
Man grows angry, becaufe I did not diftinguifh the Plays of *Seneca* the Philofopher
from the reft, and exempt him from Cen-
Survey. p. 184. fure. Why, truly I had no leifure for tri-
fling in Criticifms : And moreover, I could
not wholly excufe him; for his Rants (if
they belong to him) are fometimes as extra-
? Senec. Troad.
Act. 3. vagant as may be * .

His Parallel of *Ajax Oileus* with a late Mif-
fortune won't hold. For *Ajax* was funk in
his Blafphemy, and had his Breath ftop'd
Survey. p. 187. with a Thunderbolt : He is *no Perfon of the
Drama* ; But what then ? This Inftance is fufficient

ficient to shew the Poet's Justice, and make
an Example of the Crime.

His pretended Division of Tragedy from
Aristotle into *Moral* and *Pathetick*, is strangely
misrepresented. By this Distinction he would
make us believe, that according to *Aristotle*,
the *Pathetick Tragedy* had no regard to Morality, and Poetick Justice. But this is not
only contrary to Matter of Fact, but to the
Authority of the Citation.

For, *Aristotle* makes four Branches of his
Division of Tragedy, and not two only, as
this Author quotes him. These four kinds of
Tragedy the Philosopher forms upon the four
principal Excellencies relating to this
Art.

The first sort he calls πιπλεσμίνη, or that
which turns chiefly upon Intrigue, and Discovery; The second is the *Pathetick*, the
Beauty of which consists in the skill of
touching the Passions, and awakening Terror
and Pity to an unusual degree. Now if the
Fable was well cast, and Poetick Justice observed, as I have prov'd it often happen'd;
in this case I say, this sort of Tragedy, is e- *Survey.* p.226.
very jot as instructive, or in other words as
Moral, as any other.

The 3d sort was distinguish'd by a plain
and pompous Narration without surprize of
Incidents or Revolution of Affairs. Here the
Gods made a great part of the Dialogue,
and the Peculiarity of it lay in the Majesty
of the Presence, of the Subject and Expression.   The

Arist. de Poet.
cap. 18. The fourth is the ηθικὴ or *Moral*, so called because, as appears by the Instances, and the learned Paraphrast *Goulston*, it dealt chiefly in virtuous Examples, and Characters of Justice and Piety. In a word, the Distinction goes more upon Person, Character, and Discourse, than upon *Fable* and Event. And thus 'tis plain, that *Aristotle* was far from having any of the Surveyor's fancie's in his head : For all these kinds of Tragedy notwithstanding their Difference, were equally capable of a good *Moral*, and of adjusting Rewards and Punishments, And therefore this Philosopher was no such *inexhaustible Spring of Corruption*, no such *everlasting Source of In-*Survey. p. 195.*fection*, as this Gentleman and his terrible Rhetorick would make him.

Having now disabled his Instances of Exception, and vindicated the *Antients* ; the Design of his Attack is defeated. And his long Declamation, into which he has ramm'd Survey, p. 196. 197, & deinc. so many hard words, will recoil upon himself ; and discharge nothing but Smoke and Noise, Paper and Powder.

For by this time I suppose 'tis pretty clear that my *Satyr* (as he calls it) *does* not *come* Survey. p. 201. near *so full upon the Antients*, as *upon* the *Moderns*.

For first, As we have seen the Old Tragedians were generally unexceptionable in their *Fable* ; and when they were not, tis because they were tied down to the Models of History and Religion, upon which account both Survey p. 187, 188.

Aristotle

Ariſtotle and the *Surveyor* are willing to make them an Allowance.

Secondly, The Antient Tragick Poets were clean in their Expreſſion. And

Thirdly, They are not near ſo full of Profaneneſs and Atheiſtical Rants.

The *Surveyor* is reſolv'd notwithſtanding to produce ſome Modern Tragedies, which tho they have little to ſay, are to look boldly upon the Court, and paſs their Reſolution for their Innocence ; And here *Shakeſpear's Hamlet* is brought firſt, and a great many Words ſpent to prove the Regularity and Inſtructiveneſs of the *Fable.* But, what's all this to the Controverſy ? My Exceptions to *Hamlet* related only to his Indecencies of Language; and how handſomly the *Surveyor* juſtifies that, we ſhall ſee afterwards. However here the *Surveyor* was reſolv'd to ſet up a King of Clouts of his own making ; and then to fall on and Conquer him with great Bravery : Or, perhaps his Heart being better than his Sight, he might miſtake the *Windmill* for the Gyant.

His next Inſtance is in the *Orphan,* againſt the *Fable* of which tho I did not except, yet 'tis by no means ſo ſtaunch as he would make it. For here's no juſt Diſtinction of Fate upon the Merit of the Perſons ; but the good and bad, the innocent and guilty, fall under a common Misfortune.

Survey. p. 201, to 206.

Cleomenes

Cleomenes comes next under the *Surveyor's* Examination : This Play he taxes extreamly *Survey.*p.212. *with the want of a Moral.* And does this prove, that the *Fable* of the *Moderns* is preferable to the *Antients ?* What makes him argue on my side ? How some People's Vanity rides their Judgment! He must be throwing his Criticisms about, tho he falls upon his Friends, and weakens his Argument by his Discovery.

The Two remaining Tragedies are *Don Se-* See *View* and *Defence.* *bastian* and the *Mourning Bride.* Now he knows I have made several material Objections against these *Plays,* which he does not attempt to remove. I must tell him therefore once for all, that the Justification of the *Fable* is no Answer : For I did not charge the *Moderns* with being being Infection all over : No, they may do Execution enough without that.

Besides, the Fable by his own reasoning *Survey.*p.222. *works least sensibly,* it sleeps as it were in the Veins, and is flow in the Operation. But foul Images, and profane Discourse, are of a quicker Dispatch, and like the Plague sudden, and sure. And then the Decency, Moral Sentences, and Gravity of the *Antients* were a sort of Counterpoyson to the *Fable :* For, as the *Surveyor* observes, the *Discourse* *Survey.*p.225. *of the Antient Tragedy was frequently Moral, when the Fable was not.* To which I must add, that when the Moderns are staunch in their main *Fable,* their Episodes and Under-Character

racter are much out of Order, and encourage Vice by giving it success. He would gladly put in still for some Advantages to the *Moderns*, with respect to the *Moral*; but the Claim sticks cruelly in the making out. He mentions Three Particulars; the Two first of which are no more than one, and that is, that *View*, 142, 146, *& alib.*

The *Moderns* are never at the Expence of a Miracle to bring about a wicked Design, as the Antients have notoriously done. *Survey.*p.218.

To this I answer,

First, That he has over-charged the Antients, and multiplied his Instances beyond Matter of Fact; as appears by what I have proved already.

Secondly, In those few *Plays* where the Allegation is true, they represented the History of their Theology, they had Common Belief for their Excuse, so that it seems rather the fault of the Religion, than the Poet. And as for the *Moderns*, their standing off from this Conduct seems to proceed more from Management than Scruple; By the Liberties they take in other Cases, we have no reason to believe they declined this ill use of *Machine* out of Conscience: But because they know this Expedient won't take: The Method looks unnatural, and the Credulity of the Audience is not high enough to make it go down.

His

His Second Advantage for the *Moderns* is,
Survey. Ibid. that *their Malefactors are generally punish'd.*
The *Antients* did the same, as I have prov'd
from the Three *Greek* Tragedians. But after
all, the *Moderns* are far from being so careful
in the execution of Justice as he pretends.
For I'm mistaken if Libertines that expose
Vertue, and droll upon Religion, are not
great Malefactors. To steal Property, is not
so bad as to steal Principle; For this latter
Practice extinguishes the Notion of Right,
and makes Thieving Universal. He that destroys the Distinction of Good and Evil, is
the worst Tyrant; for he encourages all Men
to be like himself. Now these sort of *Male-*
View, &c. p. *factors* are cherished and rewarded by the
142, 146, & *Modern Stage.*
alib.

The *Surveyor* proceeding in Defence of the
Moderns, affirms, that the *Fable of every Play*
Survey p. 219. *is undoubtedly the Author's own, whencesoever*
he takes the Story, and he may model it as he
pleases; The Characters are not so, for these the
Poet is oblig'd to take from Nature.

To this I answer,

First, In contradiction to his Assertion,
That when the Poet writes from History, he
is in a great measure confin'd to Matter of
Fact, so that the *Fable* is not in his own
power to model as he pleases. This, besides
the Reason of the thing, is already granted
Survey p. 187, by the *Surveyor,* who brought *Aristotle's* Au-
188. thority

thority for the Cafe. To which I fhall add
that of *Horace*, which may be applied both
to Fable and Characters.

Aut famam fequere, aut convenientia finge, *Horat de art: poet.*
Scriptor.

Now 'tis both *Ariftotle*'s and *Horace*'s Judg-
ment, that a Tragick Poet fhould rather go *Arift. de poet: cap. 9.*
upon Fact, and known Tradition, than pure
Invention in the choice of his Subject.

Rectius Iliacum Carmen deducis in Actus, *Horat. de Art. poet.*
Quam fi proferres ignota, indictaque primus.

Secondly, 'Tis very poffible to keep an irregular *Character* under Difcipline; for *Ter-* *View, p. 34,*
rence's Strumpets don't talk Smut, and the *35, 204, 205.*
fame Conduct will hold in other Cafes. In *Defence, p. 20,*
a word, we muft not ftretch Propriety to the *21, & alib.*
prejudice of Virtue, nor make Nature a Plea
for Debauchery. But this pretence I have
fully fatisfied elfewhere.

His laft Effort upon the *Fable* of the *Antients* is, that *neither* Ariftotle *nor* Horace, *a-*
mongft all their excellent Rules for Dramatick *Survey, p.226.*
Writing, have taken the leaft notice of Poetick
Juftice. But that neither of thefe great Men
were fo regardlefs of the *Fable*, as the *Sur-*
veyor would make them, will appear from
what follows: For,

Firft,

First, Aristotle affirms, That to represent a
Person of Probity * unhappy, would not
only ' be Unpoetical, but * Scandalous, and
' Detestable : And on the other hand, to
' make a very Wicked Man successful, is
' the most improper Conduct imaginable,
' and has not so much as a jot of the due
' requisites of Tragedy in't. The first Reason
he gives for this Censure is, because such
Preposterous Management fails in a proper
Regard to Mankind *. Now, if an Unrigh-
teous Treatment of Virtue and Vice, and
Male-administration upon Merit, is in the
Opinion of *Aristotle*, a Neglect of Humane
Nature, a Scandalous Practice, and a Breach
of *Dramatick* Law, then certainly this Philosopher did not over-look the Respects of
Justice in his Preceps for Tragedy.

This, if need be, will appear farther from
the Qualifications he requires in his Hero,
who is to suffer at the latter end of the Play.
This chief Person he would have of a Mid-
dling size for his Morals, neither remarkable
one way nor t'other : He would not have
him flamingly Wicked, for then no body
would be concern'd for his Misfortune, Com-
passion would sleep, and Tragedy flag.

But then he must fall into some great In-
discretion, and be guilty of considerable Mismanagement ; He must be punish'd δι᾽ ἁμαρτίαν
μεγάλην, for some notorious failure in his Conduct ; For some Fault which he might have
prevented ; otherwise you bring him under
the

---

marginal notes:

* Ἀνδρὸς ἐπιεικεῖς.
* Μιαρὸν ἐςὶ τῦτ. De poet. cap. 13.

Ἀτραγῳδότα- τον γὸ τῦτο ἐςί.

* Οὐτε γὸ φιλάνθρωπον.

Ibid.

the Character of thofe *Virtuous Perfons,*
* whom *Ariftotle* fays 'tis fcandalous to make   † 'Επιεικᾶς.
unhappy. Thus we fee he fuffers for his
Faults, he is made a Malefactor, tho not to
the degree of falling unpited. And thus
the Example works the right way, and the
Audience is alarm'd into Caution. Thus
they are held to their Good Behaviour, and
the *paffion* of *Terror* is *purg'd* ; which advan- *Arift. de poet.*
tages could never follow if the *Hero* had no *cap. 6.*
Faults to juftifie his Misfortune. For to fee a
good Man punifh'd for that he can't help, is
the way to make the Paffions of the Tragedy
run Riot, and grow mutinous againft Providence ; and is rather an Argument for
Defpair than Circumfpection. And this may
ferve to fhew, that *Ariftotle* was not regardlefs of Poetick Juftice.

And that *Horace,* who goes upon the Plan
of the *Antients,* was of the fame mind, is
evident from his Advice to the *Chorus,* ' to
' appear for Virtue, and perform the Offices *Ut redeat mife-*
' of Friendfhip ; To recommend Juftice, and *ris, abeat for-*
   tuna fuper bis.
' pray the Gods that Fortune might follow De- *Horat. de Art.*
' fert *. Now the *Chorus,* we know, was to *poet.*
unite with the Subject, to fupport the Defign
of the *Play,* and reprefent the Sence of the
Poet. If therefore *Horace* would have the
Chorus folicit thus ftrongly for Juftice ; he
expected, no doubt, the *Cataftrophe* fhould be
govern'd by the fame Inftructions.

And thus I have endeavour'd to detect his
Calumnies upon the *Antients*, to vindicate
their *Fable*, and to difappoint him in his Pro-
ject upon the Comparifon. And alafs! if
the *Moderns* could have carried this part
of the Preference, it would have done
them but little fervice. A formal Piece of
Juftice at the end of a Lewd Play, is nothing but a Piece of Grimace, and a Politick
Hypocrify. 'Tis much fuch a ftrain of Conduct, as it would be to let a Mad Dog loofe a-
mong the Crowd, and then knock him on
the Head when he has bitten a great part of
them. And yet this poor Excufe has no pretence in Modern Comedy, where Libertinifm
comes generally off with Victory and Flying
Colours.

And to this Performance of the *Stage* the
Surveyor now leads me, and begins with the
Defence, p. 6, 7, 8. *Definition* of *Comedy:* But againft the Latitude
and Conftruction of his Interpretation, I
have argued in my *Defence*, of which, according to his Method, he takes no notice.
And by his Defcription of the Bufinefs of
Comedy, we have no reafon to expect any
good from it.

He fays the defign of Comedy is *rather*
Survey, p.232. *Civil Prudence than Morality*, and as he is pleas'd
to go on, we are not to expect it fhould *con-*
fer Grace, or mend Principles. Then as for the
P. 234. *Characters*, tho he would *not have them all Vi-*
tious, he means not juft to qualifie them for
Newgate, or *Tyburn*; But then efpecial care
must

muſt be taken, that there is no Perſon of Sobriety amongſt them : No, *they muſt be all
Men of Pleaſure* ; for if they are tainted *with
too much Honeſty*, they will diſagree *with the
Company*, and *ſpoil the Projects of the Stage*.
Well ! I perceive the *Surveyor* is reſolv'd,
notwithſtanding his Pretences to the contrary,
to make the Modern Writers of *Comedy* more
Licentious than the *Antient* ; for *Dæmones in* Rudens. Act. 4.
Plautus informs us, that the Comick Poets in ſc. 7.
his time us'd to pretend to Diſcipline, and
throw in Lectures of Morality. And tho the
Surveyor takes care to get all his Characters of
Figure debauch'd, and won't ſuffer any thing
of Conſcience or Regularity to tread the Stage,
for fear the Audience might ſuffer by the Example : Yet *Plautus* was of another mind,
for in his *Captivi* all the Characters are ſober,
and well in order, and particularly *Tyndarus*
and *Philochares*, Two young Gentlemen, are
Men of Vertue ; and ſo is *Luſiteles*, another
of the ſame Quality and Age, in his *Trinummus*.
And then as to Perſons farther advanced in
years, there are ſeveral Inſtances both in *Plautus* and *Terence*, of Behaviour not exceptionable. But our *Stage* has refined upon the old
Model : Their Characters muſt be all Libertines, their Diverſion Smut, and their Lectures, Swearing and Profaneneſs. Their Buſineſs is not to *teach Morality*, but Lewdneſs,
not to *confer Grace*, but to Debauch Nature,
not to *mend Principles*, but to deſtroy them.
Indeed, how can the Conſequence of ſuch En-
tertain-

tertainments be otherwise? where the Persons are all Libertines, where they run such lengths of excess, and balk nothing that makes a Jest. Where Profaneness is sometimes season'd with Wit, and Lewdness polish'd with turns of Fancy. Where the Infection is made Palatable, the Mischief fortified, and their Weapons Pointed, to pass the better through a Man's Body. Now, who would learn *Civil Prudence* and *Management* from such Instructions as these? where a Man will be in danger to bring away much more Vice than Discretion. Is it worth one's while to get *Caution* with the loss of Conscience? Or, Have his Pocket Pick'd only for the sake of Wit and Dexterity? Who would choose *Bedlam* for his Seat of Diversion: Or, see *Posture Clark* do his Tricks, and Act his Metamorphoses, with the Plague about him?

Survey, p.236. 'Tis true, the *Surveyor* is contented, that not only a Gentleman of *Wit*, but of *Honour* too, should be *introduced into Comedy*; but then he guards again in limitation, for he must be *a Man of wild unreclaim'd Honour.* A Man of Wild Honour! Truly, I think, no Man's Honour can be Wilder then his Notion: Honour without Probity is next to a Contradiction in Terms, and besides, 'tis good for very little. For, to speak plainly, 'tis nothing more than Pride and Fashion, and Civility to a Man's self. I don't say but Persons of Figure may be sometimes out of Order

der

der in *Comedy*, and he mifreports me in affirming the contrary * : But then this fhould not * Surv. p.238. be done without Reftrictions, and Guard of Behaviour, * And befides they fhould be * D-fence, p. 8, 10. difciplin'd accordingly. When Dramatick Gentlemen of Sence are Knaves, or Debauchees, the Poet fhould take care to make them Lofers by their Liberty : They fhould mortifie them for their Misbehaviour, treat them with Difappointment, and put them out of Countenance. And here the Misfortune ought to rife in proportion to the Quality, for fear the Figure fhould otherwife recommend the Lewdnefs.

And to do the *Surveyor* right, he is himfelf fenfible of the neceffity of this Conduct, at leaft in fome meafure. For he grants by implication, that the Poet is obliged to bring his Libertine to *a fence of his Extravagance,* Survey, p. 237. *and a refolution of Amendment.* But that even this is not done appears fufficiently in my *View,* and may be made good much farther View, p. 242, 246, & alib. from the *Plays* cited in the *Preface* of my *Defence.*

But before I pafs on, I am oblig'd to take notice of his faying, that *Fools of what Quality foever, are the proper Goods and Chattels of* Survey, p. 235. *the Stage, which the Poets may difpofe of as they think fit.*

By his favour, to make Weaknefs of Underftanding the Subject of Comick Mirth, has neither Religion nor good Nature in't : To expofe a Man for being born without Sence,

G 4 is

is a Satyr upon the Creation ; 'tis juft as reafonable as it would be to beat a Dwarf for
being under S x Foot high. Thus to make
fport with the Misfortunes of Nature, and
infult unavoidable Infirmities, is down-right
Barbarity. Befide, fuch fort of Ridicule
can cure no Diftemper, nor Recover any
Body ; Not the Patient, for he is uncapable
of Remedy ; And as for other People, they
are out of danger of the Difeafe, and therefore need no Prefervative. To proceed :

Survey, p. 239,
105, & alib.

The *Surveyor* finding the Arguments of the
View fomewhat troublefome, would gladly
throw them off upon the fcore of Declamation : As if they were only a few noify
glittering Sentences, put together to no purpofe. Now, tho I am no Pretender to the
Talent of Haranguing, yet fuppofe the Allegation was true, 'twould do him no fervice.
For Oratory is by no means inconfiftent with
Logick. No, Perfpicuity of Proof, is, as
as *Longinus* obferves, one part of the *Sublime*.
Indeed Rhetorick is nothing but Reafon well
drefs'd, and Arguments put into Order. To
affirm, That Sence won't agree with proper
and moving Expreffions, is a ftrange Con-
clufion. 'Tis as much as to fay, that a good
Suit of Cloaths is a very naughty thing :
For let it fit never fo eafie, yet if it happens
to look handfomly, 'twill be fure to weaken
a Man's Body, and take away the ufe of his
Limbs. But I muft follow him.

Ben

Ben Johnson, I took notice, never scrupled to confess, that ' 'twas the Office of a Comick View, p. 159, ' Poet to imitate Justice, and instruct to Life. 164. ' And Mr. *Dryden* at last came up to the same ' Opinion. This Rule the *Surveyor* was sensible agreed very ill with the *English* Stage. And thus finding himself streighten'd moves for new Liberty, and tho he stands by himself, had much rather bend the Rule, then reform the Practise. If you'l believe *Survey*. p. 241. him, this sort of Discipline is impracticable : For *the Licentiousness of Men of Fortune, unless it be such as brings their Understandings into question, must never be censur'd or exposed in Comedy.* That is, if a Libertine ben't a Fool, he may be as Lewd and Profane as he pleases, and yet have fair Quarter, and make a good Hand on't. Yes ; for, as the *Surveyor* continues, *how immoral and offensive this Misbeha-* *Surv.* p. 242. *viour may be to sober People, the Man must escape the Censure of Comedy, because he can't be tried in her way.* That's hard ! Why, then, if she must make Malefactors, and won't punish them, let her Court be put down. If *Sence* is a Protection to Debauchery, and the most offensive Immoralities must not be touched ; If Vice must appear only for Favour and Forage, for Parade and Diversion ; If all this Liberty is presumed on by the the Laws of Comedy, and the Privilege of the *Poem?* Then, I say, the very Definition condemns it. 'Tis a Nusance in its Nature, and Poyson in its Constitution.

I

View, p. 149. I urged there was no arguing from some
Inſtances of Favour to Vitious Young People
in *Plautus* and *Terence* ; That the Conſequence
would not hold from *Rome* to *London*, becauſe thoſe Pagan Poets had a greater Compaſs of Liberty in their Religion. To this
Surv. p. 242. his Anſwer, to make it ſhort, is, *that theſe
Poets, eſpecially* Terence, *were too great Maſters
of their own Art to take an improper Liberty, only
becauſe 'twas not dangerous.* Who told him,
it was an *improper Liberty ?* The Meaſures of
Practice are form'd upon Rules of Notion,
and Schemes of Belief : Now the Directions
for Life and Manners, are ſtrangely different
in the Diviſions of Heatheniſm and Chriſtia-
nity ; And therefore thoſe Liberties might be
proper enough in the firſt, which are intolerable in the latter. But this Objection will
be rallied afterwards, and therefore I ſhall
now purſue it no farther. But the *Surveyor*
has a ſmall Reſerve : *The Laws of* Rome, ſays
Surv. p. 242, 243. he, *were very ſevere, and required Regularity of
Life ; The* Magiſtrates *likewiſe, and Cenſors of
Manners, would never have ſuffer'd Examples
of ſuch ill Conſequence to have been produced o-
penly.* From whence he would have it follow, that if *Plautus* and *Terence had ſuſpected
the Indulgences above-mention'd, had tended any
ways to the Debauching of their Youth, they durſt
not have ventur'd them into publick View.*

To this I anſwer in a Word ; That the
Roman Magiſtrates notwithſtanding the ſeve-
rity of their Government, ſuffered the Ex-
ceſſes

eeffes of the *Pantomines*, and therefore might well
allow of much leffer degrees of Liberty in their
Comick Poets : I fay, they fuffered the *Panto-*
mimes, againft whom the *Surveyor* Declaims *Surv. p. 24, 28,*
fo heartily, and charges fo very high with *& alib.*
Scandal and Brutality. And if thefe grofs
Entertainments would go down, why fhould
they take check at the more inoffenfive fallies
of Gallantry ? As the Cafe ftood, tis no
wonder if a lucky Libertine fhould fometimes pafs Mufter.

But *Plautus* and *Terence Coppied faithfully*
from Nature and depicted Humane Life in its
true and juft proportion : Let them *depict what* *Surv. p. 243.*
they pleafe, they did not Study the worft Like-
nefs ; tho their Pencil was fometimes bold,
they fhaded many Blemifhes, and aimed at
the faireft Refemblance.

The *Surveyor* rifes in his Refolution; and
and fticks not to affirm, that if the *Images,*
anfwer Life, the foulnefs of them can never
be a Fault. So far from that, the Crime lies *Surv. p. 244.*
quite on the other Side. For to be difpleas'd
with a true Reprefentation tho' never fo hide-
ous, is no better than to *quarrel with Provi-*
dence whofe Creature Mankind is ; Say you fo,
does providence make Monfters in Vice, as
well as in Figure ? Can't a fcandalous Play
be difliked without arraigning of Providence?
I thought Wickednefs had not been the
Work of Creation, but Misbehaviour ; And
that God had made the Man, but not the
Sinner. What wretched fhifts thefe Men are
put to, to make Lewdnefs paffable ! How-

However, the *Surveyor* is refolved not to quit his Hold : He will have it that when *Nature is not wrong'd thefe Liberties* of making Vice fuccefsful, and what you pleafe befides, are an unalienable Right : It feems they are en-tayl'd upon the *Poets*, and defcend by courfe of Law, from the *Roman* to the *English Stage* : Yes, fay's the Surveyor *they have a Right to all the Priviledges of their Predeceffors.* That is a Chriftian has a clear Title to imitate all the wickednefs his Heathen *Predeceffors* have pra-ctifed before him.

In the courfe of the Argument, I prefer'd the precepts of *Horace*, to the Example of *Plautus* and *Terence*, and cited him for the contrary opinion. How can that be replies the *Surveyor*, fince *Horace draws Youth* with the fame Features and Complexion that thofe Comick Poets had done before ? And in proof of his Affertion, he produces the Picture.

Ibid.

View, p. 149.

Surv. p. 244.

Cereus in Vitium flecti Monitoribus afper, &c.

This Defcription, continues he, is *not a bare Character,* of the *Humours of young People, but a Rule to draw them by.* I agree with him : But then, as they have a Byafs to the Cha-racter, they ought to have the Confequences too : The Poet fhould make them fmart for the Prodigality of their Humour, for their Ungovernable Heats, and the Folly of their Appetites. And that this was *Horace*'s Opinion appears from the reft of his Advice * .

Surv. p. 245.

* *View,* p. 150.

But

But the *Surveyor* can't find the Obſcenities
of *Plautus* condemn'd by *Horace* ; And yet Surv. p. 246.
he is lucky enough to cite the place, ſo that
it might have been his own *Diſcovery* as well
as mine.

*At noſtri proavi Plautinos & numeros, &
Laudavere ſales ; nimium patienter utrumque,
(Nedicam ſtulte) mirati * ſi modo ego, & vos
Scimus* Inurbanum, † *lepido ſeponere dicto,
Legitimumque ſonum digitis callemus, & arte.*

* *Quia verſus Plauti non ſatis numeroſe ſcripti, & ſape obſcani ſunt.* Minell. in Loc.

Here the *Surveyor* was pretty near *Horace*'s
meaning, for he grants *Plautus*'s Raillery was
Cenſur'd becauſe his *Jeſts were Clowniſh :* And
why were they Clowniſh ? Becauſe they
were too often foul, and ſmutty ; They
were carried too far, and puſh'd to Indecency. * And that *Horace* was not for this
Broad Liberty, appears farther from his Diſ-
ſwaſive :

* *Iucivile & ſcurrile dictum,* Id.

* *Il a des plaiſanteries ſouvent outrées* Dacier in Loc. Horat. de Art. Poet. View. p. 23.

*Aut immunda crepent, ignominioſaque dicta,
Offenduntur enim, quibus eſt Equus, & pater, &
res.*

But theſe Verſes *belong to the Satyræ,* and
therefore 'tis *Legerdemain* to apply them to
the *Drama.* Not at all : 'Tis plain, *Horace*
condemns Obſcenity, and that the *Roman*
Gentry had no Reliſh for Smutty Entertainments. And if they would not allow it in
their *Ruſtick Satyræ,* where there was ſome
pretence

Surv. p. 47, 49.

pretence of Character to cover it ; 'Twould have gone down much worse, in the more Polite Diversions of Comedy.

View, p. 149. I gave a short Character from *Horace* of the serviceableness of the Antient Poets, to Government and Private Life, and that by Consequence they aim'd more at Improvement then Pleasure. This, the *Surveyor* an-*Surv.* p. 249.swers, was *but a Compliment to Poetry in general, and that Comedy was not invented in the time of Orpheus.* Granting all that ; If the Compliment was to Poetry in general, one would think it should reach to all the parts of it. And tho *Orpheus* might live before Comedy, *Horace* was long enough after it. And this is he who informs us, that the Usefulness of the Antient Poets, and the Sobriety of their Conduct, gain'd them their Reputation.

De Art. Poet. *Sic honor & nomen, divinis vatibus, atque Carminibus venit.*

As much as to say, that the Reward was fasten'd to the Merit : And that if later Poets would purchase their Fame, they must follow their Pattern.

From the Directions of *Horace* to the *Chorus*, I infer'd, that this Poet would allow no Countenance or good Fortune to an immoral Character. And foreseeing it might be replied, that Tragedy was only concern'd, I endeavour'd to remove the Objection. To this the *Surveyor* opposes the Authority of
Horace,

Horace, as if the *Chorus* was put down with *Old Comedy*. For,

Lex eſt accepta Choruſque
Tupiter obticuit ſublata jure nocendi.

De Art. Poet.

The Caſe was thus ; The *Old Comedy* in the *Chorus* had taken too much Liberty with the Government, and outrag'd Perſons of Condition by Name. Upon this *Alcibiades* had *Eupolis* thrown over-board for his *Baptæ*, and got a *Bill* paſſed, That the *Stage* ſhould at their Peril name no Body in their Satyr. ⟨*Lil. Gyrald. De Poet. Hiſt. Dial.6. p.765; 766.*⟩

This is the Law which *Horace* refers to ; And therefore his Teſtimony proves no more, than that the Liberty of the *Chorus* was ſilenc'd, which Reſtraint was conſiſtent enough with the Uſe of it.

And to prove the *Chorus* did not expire with *Old Comedy*, I produced for Evidence *Ariſtophanes*'s, *Plutus*. But againſt this Inſtance the *Surveyor* ſtarts two objections, for he'l neither admit the *Plutus* for *New Comedy* ; nor ſo much as allow it as *Chorus*. I muſt try if I can perſwade him out of his Rigour. In the ⟨*View, p. 150.*⟩ ⟨*Surv. p. 153.*⟩

Firſt place then, why muſt not the *Plutus* paſs for *New Comedy* ? 'Tis plainly not *Old Comedy*. Right, the *Surveyor* grants as much ; The *deviations*, ſays he, *in it from the former practice, make it lead up the Van of the Middle Comedy.* Now the difference between *Middle* and *New Comedy* ſeem'd ſo inſignificant to the ⟨*Surv. p. 254, 258.*⟩

learn'd

*Duplex est apud Græcos Comœdia Antiqua & Nova. Turneb in Lib. 10. Inſtit. Quinſil. cap. 1. Surv. p. 259. * Surv. p. 253.*

learn'd *Turnebus*, that he branches the *Greek* Comedy into no more than two Diviſions, *Old* and *New*. To which I may add, that the *Scholiaſt* upon *Ariſtophanes* calls the *Plutus*, a ſort of *New Comedy*. *Devit. & Script. Ariſtoph. Ed. Amſtel.*

His next objection is that the *Plutus* has no *true Chorus* : Juſt now it had none at all : But I find he flags in his Proſecution. But why is it no *true Chorus?* *Ariſtophanes* who wrote the Play, I ſuppoſe liked it well enough, and calls it a *Chorus* ; and tis ſomewhat hard his word cannot be taken ; If he did not make it as he ſhould do, he muſt anſwer for it not I. *Dacier* likewiſe affirms the *Chorus* was continued in the *Middle Comedy*. Nay the *Surveyor's* *Scaliger* confeſſes the *Chorus* was taken out ; and if ſo, one would think twas in before. But the *Chorus* ſeems to be in a Condition to defend it ſelf, and to have all reaſonable Requiſites, and Capacities ; For it conſiſts of a Plurality of Perſons, Acts in the Dialogue, and offers to ſing in the Parabaſes.

Scalig. Poet. Lib. 1. cap. 7.

Δεῖ ‍δ̀ κατόπιν Τέτων ἀδ̀ολίας ἔπιϑαι. *Chor. in Plut. Act. 5. ſc. 3.*

But after all, the *Surveyor* won't allow it to be a *legitimate Chorus*: No ! Not when *Ariſtophanes* was the Father on't, and owns the Iſſue ! Well, I can't produce the Mother, and therefore if one Side of the Genealogy won't ſatisfie, I muſt leave him. But I'm to blame for talking of theſe matters, for it ſeems I read no more of the *Plutus* than

Surv. p. 262.

the *Liſt of the Perſons of the Drama*; why then, I had a notable gueſs with me, for I have

have abstracted the *Dialogue* for some Pages *View*, p. 39.
together, as the Reader may perceive if he
pleases : I think a little more Modesty would
do this Author no harm.

My Inference from *Aristotle* (as *oblique* as *Survey*. p.263.
it is) for the Continuance of the *Chorus*, I
shall venture with his Exceptions, only ob-
serving that where he says the *Magistrates gi-* P. 265.
ving the Chorus, means nothing but paying the Ac-
tors : He should have said the *Actors* in the
Chorus ; for so *Aristotle* is interpreted by *Peti-*
tus and *Goulston*. And whereas he affirms *'tis*
certain, Menander *had no Chorus* ; He should P. 267.
have given us something better than his
bare Word for't, considering *Menander* is
lost, and there's no appealing to the Author.
If he argues, that *Menander* had no *Chorus* because his Imitator *Terence* has none, the Consequence is not good. For tho a *Chorus* is
not to be found in the Remains of *Plautus*
and *Terence*, yet *Dacier* is positive, that the
Romans made use of it in Comedy, and men- *Remarques sur*
tions the *Fabulæ Attellanæ* for an Instance. *L'Art Poetique*
D'Horace Tom.
He can't deny but that *Moliere* has reviv'd 10. p. 298.
the *Chorus* in Comedy : But then he pretends
the Poet was *in his second Infancy, and us'd*
this Expedient only as Crutches *to support the In-* *Survey*. Ibid.
firmity of his Age. But this Exception goes & p. 268.
upon a Mistake, both in the Reason, and the
History. *First, Moliere* was no such Decre-
pit Person, for he Acted in his *Malade Ima-*
ginaire not many Hours before his Death :
And, as I remember, the Writer of his Life

re-

reports him not to have outlived his Four and fiftieth year. And then, *Secondly*, That the *Chorus* is no sign of a languid, de-clining Muse is clear from *Quintilian*, who prefers the Spirit, Vigour, and Elocution of the *Old Comedy* to that of the *New*. Now, the *Chorus* the *Surveyor* grants had always a part in the *Old Comedy*.

Inst. Or. Lib. 10. *cap. 1.*

Survey. p. 268.

He would gladly know to *what end I would have a Chorus in the English Comedy:* To this I can only answer, That I am surpriz'd at his Question, having given him no manner of occasion for't.

He goes on in his Defence of the Modern Comedy, and alledges, that the *success of Libertines is not given to the Licentiousness, but to the Wit and Sence, &c. which are predominant in the Character.* To this I answer,

P. 271.

First, That to make Lewdness Fortunate and Fashionable, is a dangerous Representa-tion : For it takes off the Restraints of Shame, gives a Varnish to the Vice, and heightens the Temptation.

Secondly, Treating loose Characters with Sence and Respect, provokes to Imitation, and makes the Infection catching. Many People are more inclinable to talk Wittily, than to act Wisely. Now the Wit is gene-rally not to be come at without the Liberti-nism ; for the Matter is so contriv'd, that the Sugar and the Ratsbane must go together. The Wit, I say, lies generally in Luscious Indecencies, and Outrages of Virtue and Reli-

Religion : 'Tis brisk only becaufe 'tis bold, and rather fpits than fparkles : Its Spirits are but Lees a little alembick'd, and like fome Wood it fhines only in its Rottenefs.

Thirdly, As to his *Forgers* and *Pick-pockets* P. 272. he talks of, his Conveyance, I take it, is not very clean. If he muft make ufe of thefe Gentlemen, let his Pickpocket be feated on the *Bench,* let him appear with Figure and Equipage, fwagger in the *Court,* ridicule the Judges, and banter the Laws ; and always have a Pack'd Jury to bring him Honourably off. Let but this be done, and then we need not queftion but the Myftery of Cutting a Purfe would foon drop its ill Character, improve into a Creditable Profeffion ; and it may be, as much Studied as *Coke upon Littleton.*

I urged in the *View, &c.* That *Horace* ha- View, p. 151. ving exprefly mention'd the Progrefs of Comedy, advifed the Poet to form his Work upon the Precepts of *Socrates* and *Plato,* and the Models of Moral Philofophy ; and from hence I infer'd, that by *Horace's* Rule the Poet was oblig'd to Sobriety of Conduct, *&c.*

To this the *Surveyor* replies, That *the Lift of Qualifications mention'd by* Horace, *feem pre-* Survey, p. 275. *par'd only for Tragick and Epick Poetry.* His Reafon is, becaufe the Bufinefs feems too public, and too much rais'd for *Comedy.* But under favour, there's no need of *Buskins :* For the Defcription defcends to private Affairs, to the Regards of Blood, and the Laws of Friendfhip : Now thefe Duties, in the

H 2 Judg-

Inftitut. Lib.
10. cap. 1.
omnibus rebus,
perfonis, affecti-
bus, accommo-
datus.

Judgment of *Quintilian*, were taught no where better than in the Comedies of *Menander*; where all the Offices of Life were run through, and every Relation adjufted. To this I may add the Authority of the Learn'd *Dacier*, who underftands thefe Inftructions of *Horace*, to relate to *Comedy*. (*Tom.* 10. p. 57.)

Survey. p. 277.

The *Surveyor* makes another little ftand, and fences with the Diftinction between *Moral*, and *Poetical Manners*; affirming, that *Horace* is to be underftood of *Manners* only in the latter Sence. But by this Gentleman's favour, 'tis pretty plain, that *Horace* muft mean both; To what purpofe elfe fhould he recommend the Rules, and Writings of *Plato*, and *Socrates*? Thefe great Men gave no Inftructions about Poetry, unlefs to ftand clear on't; Nor treated *Manners* in any other fignification than that of Philofophy.

P. 278.

The *Surveyor*, who is extreamly eager to find Faults, and apt to make them, charges my *Account of Poetical Manners as deficient.* It may be fo: However, 'twas fufficient for Purpofe and Occafion. And befides, this place gave him notice of another, where there is a Defcription much as full, tho not fo tedious as his own.

View, p. 218, 219.

I complain'd, as I had great reafon, That the *Stage* made Women, fingle Women, and Women of Quality talk Smuttily: Here the *Surveyor* cries, *I run upon the wrong Scent,* argue too faft from the Premiffes, and *becaufe Modefty*

Modesty is the Character of Women, misinfer, *Surv.* p. 286, 287.
that *no Woman must be shewn without it.* Yes,
I stand by the Conclusion, That no Woman
ought to be shewn without *Modesty,* unless she
appears for Censure and Infamy, or, as
Mr. *Rymer* speaks, *to be kick'd in Comedy.* And See *Defence*, p. 10, 11, 16, &c.
even then, there ought to be a Regard to the
Audience ; and tho the Character is foul, the
Language should be clean.

But to bring single Women, and Quality
of that Sex, under these Disorders, is still
more unaccountable. 'Tis a direct crossing
upon Nature and Custom, and a breach of
Manners, both Ceremonious and Poetick.
For, do Virgins and Bawds Discourse in the
same Dialect ? Is there no difference between
Ladies and little Prostitutes ? Or, Is Rampan-
cy and Lewdness the Character of Breeding ?
If not, why is Nature thus disguis'd, and
Quality mismark'd, and all to the Disadvantage of Sobriety ? But the *Surveyor* objects,
That tho Courage is the Characteristick of the o- *Survey.* p. 287.
ther Sex, yet 'tis neither Solecism nor general Af-
front, to represent a Man a Coward. To this I
answer,

First, That Courage is not reckon'd a
Quality so essential to a Man, as Modesty to a
Woman ; The Expectation of it is not so
general, nor the Failure so monstrous ; and
therefore his Instance is not parallel.

Secondly, There are some Circumstances
and Conditions of Life, which tie this Qua-
lification faster, and as it were Incorporate it

to

to the Sex; and that is Breeding, Quality, &c.
And to argue upon his own similitude;
Tho to *represent Men sometimes as Cowards, may
be no Solecism*, yet to represent *Hercules* or
Hector, such, would be great Impropriety.
Now, Decency of Language is as much the
Character of Gentlewomen, as Bravery is of
Heroes; so that to give a Lady the nauseous
Liberties of a Procuress, degrades her in her
Quality, and is both affronting and impro-
per.

Thirdly, This Practice, as I have prov'd it,
being frequent, and without Censure upon
our *Stage*, is still more unpardonable.

Fourthly, I observ'd, that this Freedom
was a Breach of good Behaviour to the Audience, of which he is pleas'd not to take
any notice.

Survey, p.250.   The *Surveyor* urges farther, *That the Vices of
particular Women, are no Affront to the Sex in
general*; But this Excuse, were it true, without Limitation, would not serve his Turn.
For I have prov'd, That the *English Stage*
have given the Women a Coarse Character
View, p. 171, in general, and play'd their Satyr upon the
172, 173.   whole Sex.

But before I proceed, I must not forget how
the *Surveyor* takes occasion to tell us, That *in
Survey. p.288. *Plays the Characters are neither Universal nor
general*: His first Reason is, because *Marks so
comprehensive are the Impressions and Signatures
of Nature, which are not to be corrected or improv'd by us.* Now one would have thought
                                        the

the Characters would have been the better
for answering the truest proportion; and
coming up to the Standard. This appears to
have been *Horace*'s Opinion, who recommends
it as a Rule to his Stage Poet.

Respicere exemplar vitæ morumque jubebo   De Art. Poet.
Doctum imitatorem,& veras hinc ducere voces.

That is, as *Dacier* interprets him, 'Nature
' is the right Plan for *Life* and *Manners.*
' And therefore a good Poet, who has a
' mind to bring a Covetous, or Ambitious
' Person upon the Stage, will choose to form
' the Image more upon Idea, than Example;
' and Paint him rather from general Notion,
' than particular Life,

Et veras hinc ducere voces.

For this is consulting the Original, and
the way to 'give Truth, and Strength to the
' Resemblance. Whereas to draw from Par-
' ticulars in the World, is, as *Plato* speaks,
' no more than a Second-Hand Likeness, and
' but Copying at the best. In Individuals a
Quality is often cramp'd and disguis'd by
other Passions, and does not strike out to its
full extent: But an Idea considers the progress
of Inclination, makes way for Fancy and
Freedom, and gives a Character its just Com-
pass and Distinction. And therefore those
Images which are fit for Sight, should be taken
from thence.   H 4   The

The *Surveyor* objects in the next place, That *such comprehensive Marks give us no Idea of the Person Characteriz'd, but what is common to the rest of the Species, and don't sufficiently distinguish him.* But the reason of this Objection stands upon nice Ground, and will be apt to run off into unwarrantable Practice : To keep the Character within the Crowd, is the most inoffensive Method. Indeed the Distinction ought not to turn upon Persons, but Things. The Quality should be mark'd, but not the Man ; and the Vice expos'd, without pointing at the Vitious.

For to descend to Particulars, and fall to *Characterizing,* is no better than Libel, and Personal Abuse. In short, the Poet should endeavour to abstract the Fault from the *Subject,* to hover in Generals, and fly at the whole Covey : For if he once comes to single out his Quarry, he discovers himself a Bird of Prey.

His saying the *Impresses, and Signatures of Nature, are not to be corrected or improv'd, and therefore not to be meddled with,* is a great mistake. For if these *Impresses* and *Signatures,* are any better than *Jargon,* he must mean the good and bad Qualities incident to Humane Nature. Now take them either way, and his Proposition is not true. For, First, People's Miscarriages are by no means inevitable. The Blemishes in Conduct, and Character, are the Consequences of Choice. The Faults of Nature in this sence, are none of her Necessities,

fities, and therefore very capable of Correction. And then, as for the Virtues, and noble
Qualities, if they are fometimes heighten'd
above Practice, where is the harm on't? Example does not reach up to the utmoſt extent
of Power. And therefore if Nature was
ſhewn to the beſt Advantage, and ſtretch'd
to the length of her Capacity, the Pattern
might be ſerviceable, and awaken to Induſtry,
and Imitation.

We are now coming to the Parallel of the
Expreſſions, and here the *Surveyor* gives in a
Collection of *Smut* and *Prophaneneſs*, in
which he pretends the Poets of *Greece* and
Rome, are more Licentious than ours. He
acquaints us beſides, according to his Cuſto-
mary Flouriſhes, that he has ſome hundreds
of Inſtances in Reſerve. And yet after all,
he *deſires the Reader to take notice, that he does* Survey, p.292.
not charge theſe Paſſages as Faults, or Immora-
lities upon the Antients, &c. How careful he
is not to fall foul on Debauchery? He
ſeems afraid leſt the Reader ſhould miſtake
him for a Perſon that lay under ſome faint
Prepoſſeſſions of Modeſty. Yes: The Pedantry of Virtue, and the Pretences to Religion,
are uncreditable Qualities, and a Man muſt
clear his Reputation of them as well as he
can! He charges the Licentiouſneſs of the
Antients with Immorality! By no means!
That would be *foure* and *Cynical* indeed! He
underſtands himſelf better than to range
Smut, and Profaneneſs, under Immorality!
                                        Such

Such a Cenſure would recoyl upon himſelf.
If theſe Practices are Faults, then his whole
Book is little better than a Defence of Lewdneſs, and a Plea for Irreligion. The truth
of this Imputation, tho a ſevere one, is very
evident : For having brought ſeveral groſs
Inſtances of Indecency out of *Plautus*, he
juſtifies the Imitation of them ; And roundly
affirms, That ſince *Antient, and Modern Poets,
ought to be govern'd by the ſame Laws, 'tis but
reaſon, that one as well as 'tother, ſhould be al-*
Survey.p.293. *low'd the benefit of them :* That is, the benefit
of Smut and Lewdneſs. Thus the *Engliſh
Dramatiſts* are brought off without the leaſt
Blemiſh or Blot in their Scutcheon. But here's
more Comfort for them behind : For he is
P. 367. pleas'd to affirm, That *if the Paſſages of the
Antient Poets were compar'd with thoſe produced
by me out of the Moderns, the comparative Rude-
neſs, and Profaneneſs of the latter would vaniſh.*
And yet he takes particular care to inform the
Reader, That he *does not charge the Antients
with any Faults, or Immoralities upon this ſcore :*
Adding withall, That the *Moderns* ought to
have the Benefit of the ſame Liberty. From
whence 'tis plain to a Demonſtration, That
this Author has given the *Stage* a greater Latitude, and prompted them to an Improvement in Diſtraction. They may, it ſeems,
lard their Plays thicker with Obſcenities, diſ-
charge their Oaths faſter, and double their Blaſ-
phemies. Well ! I perceive Wickedneſs
would have a glorious time on't under this
Surveyor !   But

But is he fure after all, that *the Antient and Modern Poets, as Poets, are to be govern'd by the fame Laws.* Is there no difference between the Doctrines of Heathenifm and Chriftianity ? Are the Objects of Worfhip the fame in both ? And are Knowledge and Ignorance to be treated with the fame Allowance ? I thought the *Modern Poets,* as well as other People, had been under the Jurifdiction of God, Almighty, and tied up to the Laws of the *Gofpel.* But it feems the Stage is all *Franchifes,* and Privileg'd Ground : The Mufes have a particular Exemption, and the Chriftian is difpenc'd with by the *Poet.* This is the *Surveyor*'s Reafoning. However, to give him his due, he has formerly been not altogether of this Opinion. For elfewhere he tells us, That *the main bufinefs of a Chorus is* Survey.p.268, *cut off by our Religion,* which is the reafon we 269. *have no Hymns nor Anthems fung upon the Stage,* but make ufe of Smutty Songs in ftead of them. I find then by his own Confeffion, that the change of Religion has fome Influence upon the *Stage :* This was his former Judgment, but he improves by Writing, and his laft *Will* muft ftand.

The *Surveyor* in his *Parallel,* blackens the *Antients* moft unmercifully, and fwells their Charge beyond all Truth and Proportion. This is done to make the Moderns look the more tolerable, and keep them the better in Countenance. But a little Pains will ferve to wipe off moft of the Spots, and reftore
them

them to their Complexion. And here I can't help obferving, That let the Antients be as faulty as may be, the *Surveyor* fhould by no means pretend to difcover it : For he has already fully acquitted the *Greek* and *Roman Dramatifts* of all Imputations of In-decency, and roundly pronounced, That tho the *Mimi* were fcandaloufly Lewd, the *Drama* was not at all. But to return :

Survey. p. 23, 24.

Before he draws out upon the Old Poets, he endeavours to defend his *Ophelia.* And here he tells us a long Story, how *warrantable her Love was*, how *artfully manur'd*, and ftrongly *forc'd up* ; And by his Defcription, one would think he was raifing a Muskmelon. But then, as ill Luck, and the Poet would have it, her Humble Servant *Hamlet killing her Father by miftake, and counterfeiting Mad-nefs*, ruined all. This Misfortune *muft needs make horrible Convulfions in a Mind fo tender*, and, as the *Surveyor* Compliments the Ladies, *in a Sex fo weak.* Well : Her Father was kill'd, *&c.* But, what then ? Muft fhe needs Lament in Smut, and pay her Refpects in Diftraction ? Are Lufcious Expreffions the Natural Effect of *Deep Sorrow*, and can't fhe appear *Tender*, without being Rotten ?

Survey. p.293, 94

P. 294.

P. 296.

However, to do the *Surveyor* right, he has produced the Exceptionable Lines, for 'twas the *Song* which I complain'd of. And this, if you'l believe him, is fo innocent, that there's *no fear of offending the Modefty of the moft Chaft Ear.* I'm forry he feems to have loft

P. 295.

loft the very Notion of Decency. He's more to blame for *tranfcribing*, then *Ophelia* was for Singing this Ditty, becaufe he wants her Madnefs for his Excufe. Now 'tis but an untoward Bufinefs, when a Man is the worfe for being in his Wits.

But now the *Surveyor* is come to his Diffection of the *Old Poets*: And here his Reading upon the Body is admirable; and to magnifie his Skill, he fpies out more Difeafes then e're the Patient died of. He often arraigns an Innocent Expreffion, and when 'tis not fo, his Paraphrafe is much groffer than the Text. For 'tis generally his way when he lights upon a fore place, to make it much worfe for the Dreffing. However, he feems to have gotten a very agreeable Subject: For his Ink flows amain, and his Invention grows very copious: He feems to Swim at his Eafe, and his Fancy plays down the Stream, and tumbles in the Mud, with great Satisfaction.

He begins with *Sophocles's Antigone*: This Lady he pretends makes fome Intemperate Difcoveries, and does not keep up to the Decencies of Sex, and Condition. To underftand fomething of the *Fable*, this *Antigone* was by King *Creon* her Uncle, fentenc'd to be fhut up in a Cave, and ftarv'd to death, only for burying her Brother *Polynices* contrary to the King's Order: She was likewife contracted to his Son *Hæmon*. Now, tho fhe had ftood firm againft the Menaces of

Creon,

Creon, and fhewn her felf Brave and good
Natur'd to an extraordinary pitch; yet
when fhe comes to be led to Execution, her
Fortitude gives way a little to the Tendernefs
of her Sex; fhe breaks out into fome natural Starts of Concern, and according to the
Cuftom of that Age, and the Eaftern Countreys, * laments her dying young and fingle.
But fhe makes a fhift to govern her Language,
and keeps her Paffion from boiling over. I
fhall tranfcribe his moft ferviceable Line, in
which fhe Complains of the Difappointment
of her Fortune, and that fhe muft go off.

* Judg. 11.
v. 37.

> Ἄλεκτρον ἀνυμέναιον ἔτε τῦ γάμε
> Μέρῷ λαχῦσαν.

That is, that fhe muft die fingle, and be
crofs'd in her Love with *Hæmon* : Upon
whom, tho the *Surveyor* overlook'd it, 'tis
plain fhe had *fettled* her *Affection*. For when
Creon threatned to break the Contract, fhe
difcovers her Regards to *Hæmon* in a very
intelligible, tho decent Expreffion.

Survey, p. 300.

> Ω φίλταθ αἷμων, ὡς σ' ἀπιμάζει πατὴς.

His next Inftance is *Electra*, who goes a little
upon the Complaint of *Antigone*.

Survey. p. 301.

> ———— Ἄτεκνῷ
> Τάλαιν ἀνύμφευτῷ αἰεν οἰχνῶ
> Δακρυσι μυδαλέαι

This

This Lady, we muſt underſtand, had ſeen her Father Murther'd, by her Mother and *Ægiſthus* ; She was likewiſe ill treated in the Family, and had no Body to take care of her Intereſt, and make good the Expectations of her Birth : She had none but her Brother *Oreſtes* to depend on, and his long abſence made her afraid ſhe was forgotten. In ſhort, ſhe was impatient for his return, and ſeems *Sophoc. Elect.* rather to wiſh for Protection and Revenge, *Act. 2. & alib.* than a *Settlement*. And were it otherwiſe, the Expreſſion is perfectly inoffenſive. And thus *Sophocles* ſtands diſengaged without difficulty; And had the *Engliſh Stage* been thus reſerv'd, they had ſav'd me the trouble of a whole *Chapter*.

As for *Æſchylus* the *Surveyor* does not ſo much as offer at him ; ſo that there's Two of the Three *Greek* Tragedians ſecur'd. But

Euripides is now ſet to the Bar, and terribly handled for giving this Line to *Polyxena* when ſhe was going to be ſacrificed. *Survey. p. 301.*

———Ἄπειμι, δὲ κάτω
Ἄνυμφ⊙, ἀνυμέναι⊙ ὧν μ᾽ ἐχρῶ τυχεῖν.

That is, ſhe was going to die unmarried, and without being diſpos'd of according to the Privilege of her Condition. This *Complaint* is in the *Surveyor's* Aggravation very *unreaſonable*. He grows very Tragical upon the occaſion, taxes the Princeſs with *Incon-* *Survey. p. 302.* *tinence*, meanneſs of Spirit, and an intemperate
rate

rate defire of engaging with the *Conquerour* of her Country, tho at the difadvantage of being his Slave. But this Lady is wrong'd by the *Surveyor*, the Cafe is mifreported, and, as it fometimes happens, the Indictment is fet forth with a great deal more noife than Law. Let the Lady fpeak for her felf. Now *Eurip. Hec. Act.* in this very *Scene*, fhe laments the Misfor- *2.* tunes of her Family ; and lets us underftand, that her Birth gave her juft Pretences to be difpos'd of to a Monarch : But now the Ruine of her Country had chang'd the Pro- fpect, and made Marriage her Averfion : She could now expect nothing but that fome little Slave fhould be forc'd upon her.

Λέχω ἢ τἀμὰ Δῦλ☉ ἀνετὸς ποϑέν
Χεανεῖ, τυράννων περ ϑεν ἠξιωμένα.

Eurip. p. 13, And therefore fhe goes boldly to the Altar, *14.* congratulates her Murther, and is pleas'd with *Ed. Cantab.* the Refcue of Death : She is glad not to fur- vive her Greatnefs any longer ; and fays, Life is over-purchas'd upon the Terms of Igno- miny. In a word, fhe is fo far from defer- ving the *Surveyor's* Cenfure, that when fhe comes to the Block, fhe makes Decency her laft Care, and expires in the Character of her Condition.

Ibid. p. 20. Πολλὰ` πρόνοιαν εἶχεν εὐσχήμως πεσεῖν.

Th

The *Surveyor* is now for perfecuting her Sifter *Caffandra*, and one would almoft think, that he had, like *Juno*, a fpite to the whole Family.

This Lady he blames for being too for-ward in difcovering her Satisfaction at the News of *her Match* with *Agamemnon* ; but, *Surv.* p. 305, 6, 7.

Firft, Here is not fo much as the leaft Exceptionable Expreffion ; but the Language is inoffenfive to the moft exact Nicenefs : And therefore he has blackn'd the Page with *Greek* to no purpofe.

Secondly, Caffandra's forwardnefs to comply proceeded purely from her Revenge. Being in a Prophetick Fit, fhe forefaw this Match would prove fatal to *Agamemnon* and his whole Family. And tho fhe knew her felf was fhortly to be Murther'd, yet the pro-fpect of revenging her Country, and de-ftroying her greateft Enemies, made her run into Tranfport, and defire her Mother to Congratulate her Happinefs.

Κτενῶ γὰρ ἀυτὸν, κἀντιπορθήσω δόμες, Ποινὰς ἀδελφῶν κ πατρὸς λαβῦσ᾽ ἐμῦ. *Troad.* p. 145.

And after having enlarg'd upon the Mif-fortunes of the *Greeks*, and fhewn how glo-rioufly the *Trojans* died in the Defence of their Country, fhe perfwades *Hecuba* not to afflict her felf ; for now, fays fhe, I am going to make the General a full Return, and to finifh his Ruine.

I   — Τῦς

Ibid. 146.

——Τῆς γὰρ ἐχθίςτς ἐμοὶ,
Καὶ σοὶ, γάμοισι τοῖς ἐμοῖς διαφθερῶ.

Survey p.306
308.
But *Caſſandra*, in the *Surveyor*'s Opinion, ſhould not have been ſo forward to ruſh upon her own Diſhonour. To clear this, we muſt underſtand, that *Caſſandra* was under extraordinary Circumſtances : ſhe was poſſeſs'd both by *Apollo*, and a very Governing Paſſion beſides : Now 'tis no wonder if the Tranſports of Prophecy and Revenge, ſhould make her a little overlook other Conſiderations. But this Reaſon apart, it does not appear that *Caſſandra* was forc'd upon any Diſhonourable Troad. p. 143. Engagement ; For the Favour of a Prince was not, as *Talthybius* tells her Mother, unreputable at that time of day. *Polygamy* was then the Practice of ſeveral Countreys, and particularly the Cuſtom of her own, as appears from the Diſcourſe between *Hermione*, * Androm. p.
301, 302. and *Andromache* *.

As for old *Hecuba*, I confeſs *Euripedes* has given her a Luſcious Expreſſion to make her Intereſt with *Agamemnon*. But then it does not come up to the pitch of Scandal of many Paſſages of the *Engliſh* Stage : 'Tis meer Baſhfulneſs to ſome of their Songs, and Courtſhip : And thus out of Nineteen *Plays* in *Euripides*, the *Surveyor* has made a ſhift to furniſh one paſſage out of Order. But inſtead of producing One out of Nineteen, I could return him Nineteen out of One, from the *Moderns*, were it convenient. But

But as the *Surveyor* reports the Cafe, *Euri-aides* has fomewhat farther to anfwer for. 'tis true his Tendernefs is fuch that he refu-fes to give in particulars; but the Reader is referred in general to the exceptionable Plays. Well: *Dolus latet in Generalibus* is a true fay-ing. The *Surveyor* has hid himfelf in a Fo-lio, and now is fafe enough: He loves like *Virg. Æneid. 8.* *Cacus* to make a Smother in his Cave, to con-ceal his foul Play. Indeed I think the Smoke is his beft Defence, and the finding him out the hardeft part of the Enterprize. To come up with him.

His Inftance in *Hermione* and *Andromache*, *Surv. p. 312. Androm. p. 301,302,303.* is altogether fhort. They chide, 'tis true, a little too warmly for their Quality, if we Breed them by our own Times; but nothing foul or diforderly paffes between them: And as for *Creufa*, his quarrel with her is nothing but ill-will: For fhe does not in the leaft run her *Jon. p. 317, 333, 334. p. 351.* felf a ground in her Story, but relates her Misfortune with great refervednefs. Neither does her Son *Jon* put any uncivil Queftion to her. His Modefty is very defenfible, if not his Manners: Tho' even in this latter re-fpect the young People upon the Stage are now more free with their Parents than this comes to. And laftly, *Electra* is innocent of the Accufation he brings againft her. 'Tis true, fhe encourages *Oreftes* to kill his *Mother*, but then fhe ftands clear of Indecency, and fays nothing in that refpect, misbecoming her Character: So far from that, that fhe

won't

won't so much as mention the Debaucheries of
Ægyſtus; no not when ſhe was recounting
his other Villanies, and triumphing in his
being Diſpatch'd. She runs over his guilt
in Murther and Injuſtice, but when
ſhe came to his Lewdneſs, ſhe cuts off her
Story, and declares it, no fit Subject for a
ſingle Lady.

Electr. p. 427, 428.

Ἃ δ' εἰς γυναῖκας, παρθένῳ γὰρ ἐ καλὸν
λέγειν, σιωπῶ, γνοείμως δ' αἰνίξομαι.

The *Greeks* being now diſmiſs'd, *Seneca*
Surv. p. 314. comes on for another Hearing. And *Phædra*
in *Hippolitus* is pitch'd upon for a Character
of Misbehaviour : But the *Surveyor* knows I
View, p. 25. excepted againſt her Management my ſelf ;
And cenſured the freedom of her Diſcovery,
only with this abatement, that her Language
was under Diſcipline : And that the latter
part of my aſſertion was no leſs true than the
former, will eaſily be underſtood by any one
that reads the Poet in himſelf, and not in
the *Surveyor*'s Paraphraſe: But it ſeems the
Nurſe runs over in her Expreſſion, and does
Survey. p. 317. not ſuit her Language to her Advice ; And
here the force of the Charge lies all in one
Word, (for the reſt is only for ſhow;) In
an anſwer to which, we may obſerve that
Words don't always keep cloſe to their firſt
Signification ; but grow ſometimes the worſe
for the wearing : And that the Old *Romans*
had an Idea different from the *Surveyor*'s, in the
Expreſ-

Expreſſion under debate, appears ſufficiently
from *St. Hieroms* Epiſtles, who uſes it without ſcruple.

Epiſt. adverſ. Helvid. & alib.

I obſerv'd that we had no Courting in *Seneca*, except in the *Hercules Furens*, where the

View, p. 25,

Tyrant *Lycus* addreſſes *Megara* very briefly,
and in modeſt remote Language. This the
Surveyor does not deny ; but then he pretends to give an Inſtance of *Lycus's* Misbehaviour to *Amphitrio*, I ſhall tranſcribe his
Quotation for the Reader.

> *Jovi dediſti conjugem regi dabis.*
> *Et te Magiſtro non novum hoc diſcet Nurus,*
> *Etiam viro probante meliorem ſequi ;*
> *Sin copulari pertinax tædis negat,*
> *Vel ex coacta nobilem partum feram.*

Herc. Fur,

Now am I at a loſs to what purpoſe theſe
fine Verſes were cited. It muſt be for the
Learning in the Language. Yes : He may
poſſibly, like ſome Patients, fancy the Phy-
ſick Works much the better, for the *Latin* in
the Bill.

But he goes on with wonderful Courage,
as if he was reſolv'd to ſwagger the *Reader*
out of ſome part of his Sences : *If theſe Al-
lowances,* ſays he, *may be made,* (meaning for the
laſt Citation) *I'le engage to prove, there never

Surv. p. 319,

was an immodeſt thing ſaid upon the* Engliſh
Stage. Certainly this Author has a Taſt peculiar to himſelf ! One would think he ſhould
be better Read in Smut, by his Talent in

Writing

Writing it. I'm afraid this Ignorance is all affected : And that he has gotten the trick of shrinking up his Understanding, as they say some Beggars do their Arms upon occasion.

Survey, p. 319. He tells me, *I forgot the shameful solicitations which* Phrædra *us'd to corrupt* Hippolytus. He knows I took notice of *Phrædra's* Irregular Freedoms, but then, tho her *Solicitations*

Ibid. *are shameful*, they are not Smutty. He would perswade the *Reader*, that *Seneca's Agamemnon* is stock'd with Curiosities of this kind. And yet there is but one Line which looks the least that way : and that is *Clytemnestra's* Reproach to *Ægystus*, in which she tells him, That his Lewdness was the only Proof of his Manhood.

Agam. Act. 2.　*Quem venere tantum scimus illicita virum.*

Now this Rebuke is so comparatively Civil, that were it in some of our Plays, the Modesty of it would almost put it out of Countenance, and kill the Expression.

The *Surveyor* has hitherto found but small Returns from his Enquiry. He has rang'd over a great deal of Ground, and Quarter'd the Fields of *Greece* and *Italy*. But all this Questing has sprung but very little *Game*. However, he seems extreamly busie, and by his motion would make you believe every Butterfly was worth the *setting*. *Who-*

Survey. p. 313, *ever,* says he, *consults the Passages amiss in* So-
319. phocles *or* Euripides, *or Censures with the Al-*
lowances

lowances made to Seneca, *will find the most exceptionable Passages in our Poets, whether Comick or Tragick, very excusable upon a fair Construction.*

The *Moderns* compar'd with the *Greek* Tragedians and *Seneca,* in Point of Decency, and Sobriety of Language ! He may almost as well compare *Aristophanes* with *Terence,* and the Sixth *Æneid* of *Virgil,* with the Sixth *Satyr* of *Juvenal.* The *Moderns !* who not only glance, but dwell upon an ill Subject, bandy it between the two Sexes, and keep it up to shew their Skill in the Exercise. Yes : They love to flourish upon Lewdness, to refresh it with Repetition ; and beat it out into Length and Circumstances. Sometimes to distinguish a foul Thought, they deliver it in *Scripture Phrase,* and set it in Gold to make it sparkle the better. In short, they omit nothing to explain the Mystery, and cultivate the Interest of Debauchery : Nothing that may fortifie the Poison, and make it more Poinant and Palatable. To lay their Disorders before the *Reader,* were the Sight proper, would swell into a Book, and be a tedious Undertaking. 'Twould be Infamy of Bulk, and Voluminous Distraction ; not to be scan'd by the Line, but weigh'd by the Pound. Such Plays are much more fit for the Solemnities of *Flora* and *Ceres,* than the Entertainments of those who are *Baptiz'd.* 'Tis almost pity they han't a set of *Pantomimes* to do justice to the Subject, and Dance up to the Spirit of the *Dialogue.*   I 4   The

Survey, p. 327, 328. The *Surveyor* pleads for *a Diſtinction between the private Sentiments of the Man, and the publick ones of the Poet, and that the Liberties of a Character ought not to be laid to the Charge of the Dramatiſts that repreſents them.* This Author muſt think his pleaſure, but *Quintilian* was of another mind ; who lets us know, that *Afranius*, a Vitious Comick Poet, diſcover'd

* Mores ſuos faſ-ſus. Inſt:t. Orat. Lib. 10. cap. 1. his Practice in his *Plays.* * Indeed nothing is more natural than for a Man's Fancy to flow into his Ink, and when he can, to make his Buſineſs his Diverſion. Farther : A Poet that writes looſely can never be ex-cus'd, for this is done either out of Inclina-tion, or Intereſt : If the firſt, he's a Perſon of no Sobriety, if the ſecond, of no Con-

Defence, p. 10, 11, &c. ſcience : As for the Plea from the *Nature* and *Propriety of Characters*, 'tis anſwer'd already in my *Defence*, but the *Surveyor* was reſolv'd to jog on, and overlook it.

The *Surveyor* in his Examination of *Plau-tus*, ſays, I *may bluſh for my Defence* of this Poet, for affirming his Cenſurable Paſſages

Surv. p. 328. *are very moderate*, as the World goes, and *that ſeveral of our ſingle Plays ſhall far outdo all this put together.* Now tho this may be true in the compaſs he has given it, yet 'tis much more than I affirm'd. But this Author, ac-cording to his cuſtom, has extended my Aſ-ſertion to the whole Works of *Plautus*, which

View, p. 16. relates only to the Miſbehaviour of *Women*. And in this ſence of the Compariſon, I ſtill defend *Plautus*, and in Proof of the Point appeal

appeal to the *Old Batchelour*, the *Soldie's For-tnne*, and several other *Englijh Plays*.

The *Surveyor* opens the Case farther against *Plautus*, and presses the Particulars of the Charge. And first his *Amphitruo* is oaded with a heavy Accusation. But the bet on't is, here's a mistake of the *Person*, wich is enough in all Conscience to quash the Indictment. That Rankness of Language which the *Surveyor* charges upon *Plautus*, is all *Interpolation*, and belongs to another *Author*. Now as the Poet has no reason to answer for what does not belong to him, so these *ungenuine Additions* were particularly xcepted by me. My Adversary, if he writes a-wake, must needs know these decent Quotations were nothing to his purpose. But possibly the Nosegay was made up, for a Curiosity to the *Reader*, and to oblige his own Smelling : And to make *Plautus* amends for giving him more then his due, he's resolv'd to take something from him : For at the latter end of *Amphytrio*, he slides away the word *facere*, * which quite alters the sence, and makes *Compliance* sound up to obscenity. But this is no wonder, for I observe the *Surveyor* is mightily light-finger'd this way and generally steals off the Modesty of an Author. And to aggravate the Theft, the Motive is more Malice, than Necessity : For he does not filch, to make use of his Neighbours Goods, but to destroy them.

Surv. p. 329, 330.

View, p. 18.

Mea vi subacta est facere.
Amph. Act. 5 Sc. 2.

His

Hi Objection against the Morality of the Dialogue between *Demænetus* and *Argyrippus* in the *Asinaria*, is out of the Question: I warranted no farther than the *Expression*, nor that neither, but with reference to the *Moderns*.

His next Instance is in the *Curculio*, where *Phædromus* and *Planesium* salute each other too egerly: It may be so; But then we may observe, they had not seen one another for some time, and the Visit was made with difficulty: And under such Circumstances, had they been both of the same Sex, they might have discover'd some Affection extraordinary. However he can't say the Expression is foul, * *View*, p. 16. and i it was, 'tis a *Slave* that speaks it, and so nohing to his purpose.

View, p. 17. To shew the Comparative Modesty of *Plauts*, 'I took notice, that the *Slaves* and 'Pandars who had the greatest Liberty, sel- 'don play'd their Gambols before Women; 'tha there are, as I remember, but four In- 'stances to the contrary; and that even there, 'the Women these Men discourse with, are Two 'of hem *Slaves*, and the third a Wench.

Surv. p. 334. Hre he *is sorry for my want of Memory*, but I hare much more reason to condole with him for the loss of his own. For *Olympio*, upon whom he would make his Advantage, will do him no service, the Liberties of this Slave in the *Casina* are expresly barred both by Name and Play, and stand first in the List of the Exception. I grant *Cleostrata* urges

Olympio

Olympio to tell the Story, but then tho the *View*, p. 17.
Drift of her Fancy may be amiſs, the Com-
plexion of her Language is bright, unleſs in
one Line , which, if not interpreted to
her Ignorance, is no more then a double *En-* *Survey*, p 337.
tendre. *Artemona's* Allegory in the *Aſinaria*
is ſomewhat leſs offenſive than this, tho
none of the moſt reſerv'd. Thus he has
made a ſhift to muſter up two exceptionable
Sentences of Women of ſome Conſideration
in *Plautus*. But alaſs ! What are theſe to the
repeated and Luſcious Freedoms of *Elvira*, *Spaniſh-Friar.*
of the Ladies in the *Country Wife*, of *Belinda*, *Old Batch.*
and *Lady Plyant*, of *Narciſſa*, and *Lady* *Double-Dealer.*
Fool in Faſhion.
Dunce. Not to mention a great many others. *Soldiers Fortune.*
Here the Weeds are extreamly rank, and
thick ſet : And were they worth the gather-
ing, the *Reader* might be plentifully furniſh'd
for a little pains.

The *Surveyor* has ſomething farther with
Artemona, and pretends *her Frankneſs gave her*
Slave Paraſitus *the boldneſs to put a very untu-*
ward Queſtion to her. 'Tis this,

Poſſis ſi forte accubantem tuum virum con-
  ſpexeris,
Cum corona amplexum amicam ſi videas cog-
  noſcere ?

Of theſe Lines he gives a foul and miſtaken
Tranſlation, and which is clearly confuted
both by the *Text* and *Notes*. Every body
knows Beds and Garlands were for Eating and

Publick Entertainment. And then *Gremio jacuit nova nupta mariti* was ufual enough: This was fomewhat of the Cafe of the Hufband *Demenetus*, who was difcover'd at Supper with his Son, and his Wench. And that the Appearance was fair, is evident from the Slaves Advice to his Miftrefs: He defires her to ftay a little for Information about their Behaviour:

> *Paras : Hem tibi Hominem : Art. perii !*
> *Par. paulifper mane.*
> *Aucupemus ex infidiis clanculum quam rem gerunt.*

Afinar. Act. 5. fc. 2. And upon the immediate progrefs of the Story, the old Man, the young one, and the Woman, Drink, and Difcourfe all together.

I obferv'd farther to the Advantage of *Plautus*, That ' his Men who talk intemperate- *View, p. 16.* ' ly are generally Slaves, adding, that ' I thought *Dordalus* the Pander, and *Lufiteles* a young Gentleman, were the only ' exception: And this latter was only guilty ' of one over airy Expreffion. But it feems the *Surveyor* is fomewhat fharper at thefe Enquiries, and after his rummaging over 20 Comedies has catched *Peripleĉtimines* tripping in *Mil. Glor. Act. 5.* one Word; and that too ufed by way of reproof. Now, that the Expreffion, tho out of order, is not fo grofs as he would reprefent it, appears from *Lambin's Note* upon the

Epilogue

Epilogue to the *Captivi*: And from *Chremes*'s
Reprimand of *Clitipho* in *Terence*. * To conclude this Matter, what *Periplectimenes speaks*,
the Hoſteſs in *Bartholomew Fair Aɛts*, and
that, I take it, is ſomewhat more foul, and
expreſſive.

Once more and *Plautus* is diſmiſſ'd. I affirm'd, that this *Poets Prologues* and *Epilogues*
were inoffenſive. This the *Surveyor* confeſſes
is a great Point, but ſeems to think it cann't
be carried. But here the *Reader* may pleaſe
to obſerve, that the Diſpute turns only upon
Indecency of Language, for I never intended
to vouch the Doɛtrine, and Morals of *Plautus*: And thus the *Epilogue* in the *Aſinaria* is
nothing to the *Surveyor*'s purpoſe, being perfectly clean in the *Expreſſion*. As for the E-
pilogue of the *Captivi* 'tis all in Defence of
Virtue, as well as the *Play*; And the *Aɛtors*
urge their Modeſty, as an Argument for Favour to the *Audience*. 'Tis true they plead
their Merit in one ungovern'd Expreſſion;
to which, in the Caſe of *Periplectimenes*, I
have ſpoken already. His remaining Objeɛtion is againſt the *Epilogue* in the *Caſina*.
And here I grant the Principle is ill enough,
but that is foreign to the Queſtion. But for
any other Objeɛtion, I can't perceive the
ſtrength of it. For, as to the laſt Line, upon
which I ſuppoſe he founds himſelf, this Sentence ſeems rather to contain an ill Wiſh, and
a Menace of Diſappointment, than any thing
elſe. * Beſides; As to Debauch't Principle,
the

* *Heauton. Aɛt.*
3. *S.* 3. *Ed. in*
uſum Delphin.

View, p. 17.

Surv. p. 340.

Survey. p. 342.

p. 343.

Surv. p. 341.

* *Vid. Donat.*
in Loc.

the *Prologue* to the *Plot and no Plot*, is as bad
as 'tis possible , and over and above much
more scandalous in Language, than the *Epilogue* to *Plautus*'s *Casina* ; In which the Disadvantage is shaded, and the Expression made
more remote.

And can the *Surveyor* now find in his heart
to compare the *Prologues* and *Epilogues* of
Plautus with those of the *Moderns* ? * Is the
Decency and Complexion the same in both ?
A Man must have a great Command of his
Blood, to affirm this without Blushing ; And
be almost as much a Master of his Face, as
he is of his Conscience.

As for *Terence*, he is so Staunch and Regular, that there's no medling with him : No,
The *Surveyor* does not think fit to attack this
Poet ; but leaves him as a standing Reproach
upon the *English Stage*.

I must now follow him in his Remarks
upon the *Chapter of the Abuse of the Clergy*. ,

And here his Spleen against the Church disorders him extreamly, and indeed almost
throws him into Fits. He would gladly say
something to purpose against the Clergy, but
the Subject fails him. This makes him rail
most unmercifully ; for Spight and Impo-
tence together are generally very Clamorous
and Impertinent.

To shew the unreasonableness of the Stage-
Scurrilities upon the *Clergy*, I endeavour'd to
make out the Right this *Order* had to Regard,
and fair Usage.

First,

* See *View*,
p. 13.

Survey, p. 344.

View, p 127.

First, Becaufe of their Relation to the Deity, ' where I obferv'd that Chriftian Priefts ' are the Principal Minifters of God's King- ' dom : They Reprefent his Perfon, Publifh ' his Law, Pafs his Pardons, and Prefide in ' his Worfhip.

I thought thefe things had been fo plain that they needed no confirmation, but fince the *Surveyor* contefts the Point, I fhall briefly make it good. Now, I defire to know of the *Surveyor*, what it is to Reprefent another? Is it not to be his Agent, and to Manage his Affairs by vertue of his Authority? And does not the Prieft Seal Covenants in God's Name? Does he not Baptize by Commiffion, *St. Math. 28.* and Exercife part of that Power which our *19.* Saviour had upon Earth? The *Surveyor's* Ob- *St. Joh. 20.* jection upon this Head is amazingly ridicu- *21.* lous : For by his reafoning no Man can *Reprefent the Perfon of God*, without being *poffeffed of the Divine Attributes*, and able *to fu-* *Survey. p. 346,* *ftain the Figure of Omnipotence.* As much as *347.* to fay, That a Prince can't fend another as his Ambaffadour, unlefs his Perfon, Prerogative and Appearance, is equal to his own. And therefore if the Ambaffadour falls fhort of his Mafter in the Advantages of Body, or Mind, in the Extent of his Dominions, or the Magnificence of his Retinue ; If any thing of this happens, let the Credentials be what they will, the Characters it feems finks, and the Reprefentation becomes impoffible. This is ftrong Reafoning, I confefs, for it almoft

moſt argues the World in Pieces. At this
rate Princes muſt Travel to keep the Peace,
and Tranſact all their Matters by Interview,
and Perſonal Viſit : For a *Plenipotentiary* is a
dangerous thing : They can't prefer a Subject
to an Embaſſy, without communicating their
Royalty, and making an Equal to themſelves.
And thus the *Surveyor* has gone a great way to-
wards breaking the Correſpondence of *Chriſten-
dom*. Farther, I thought the *Surveyor* would have
allow'd *Angels*, at leaſt, for their Name ſake,
to have Repreſented God almighty : But by
this Reaſoning *Michael* himſelf is ſtruck out
of Capacity, and the higheſt Order of Spirits
unqualified for the Office : For no Created
Being has any of the *Divine Attributes*, nor
which is more, can have them.

Survey, p. 347, 348. He ſays the Regards that I inſiſt on for the
Prieſthood, belongs to *the Governours of the
Church*. Now, tho he mayn't know it, Prieſts
are Governours, within their Precinct ; They
have *Regimen Animarum,* the Guidance of Souls,
and the Concerns of Eternity in their Care,
and that one would think were none of the
leaſt Intereſt of the Pariſh. I grant *Theatrum*
is a hard Word to conſtrue, but I fancied
the *Surveyor* might have known the *Engliſh* of
Rector well enough. By this time, I hope,
the *Repreſentation* may be allow'd. But then
as to the Authority of *publiſhing the Laws of
God, paſſing his Pardons*, and *preſiding in his
Worſhip*, theſe Privileges, he ſays, were pecu-
Survey, p. 348. liar to the *Apoſtles*. But his Affirmation a-
part,

part, the Holy Scriptures teach us, That *the People are to seek the Law at the Priest's Mouth, for he is the Messenger of the Lord of Hosts.* And the Church of *England* in her Form of *Ordination* gives the Priest Authority to *preach the Word of God,* and *to Minister the Holy Sacraments;* And which in her *Articles* she denies to belong to the Supream Civil Power: And as for the Power of *Passing Pardons,* and giving Absolution, 'tis founded upon that Solemn Commission given by our Saviour. *As my Father hath sent me, even so send I you, whosesoever sins ye remit, they are remitted unto them, and whosesoever sins ye retain, they are retain'd.* And can any one imagine that Words so plain in the Expression, and so solemn in the Occasion, are void of Weight and Signification? Not to mention the right they imply of Admitting into the Church, and Excluding from it; Not to mention this, they must amount to this Meaning at the lowest, That those who neglect this Ordinance of God, and refuse to apply for Absolution to Persons thus Authoriz'd, shan't have their Sins forgiven, tho otherwise not unqualified. And thus, to put a resembling Case, a Malefactor can't have the benefit of the Prince's Pardon unless it passes the Seals, and runs through the Forms of Law. And that this Power was not peculiar to the Apostles, but design'd for a standing Advantage, and settled upon the Successions of the Hierarchy; is plain by the Doctrine, and practice of our

Malach. 2. 7.
Art. 37.

St. Joh. 20. 21, 23.

K   own

own Church: For at the Ordination of
Priests the Authority of *Remitting* and *Retaining* Sin, is confer'd in the same Words,
Whosoever Sins ye remit, &c. And in the
Office for the *Visitation for the Sick*, the Priest
making express mention of his *Authority* from
our Saviour, absolves the Penitent *from all
his Sins, in the Name of the Father, the Son,
and the Holy Ghost.*

And as this Authority of the Priest is thus
fully maintain'd by the *Church*, so 'tis no less
acknowledg'd by the *State :* For the Book of
Common Prayer, with the *Form* of *Ordination,
&c.* stands upon a bottom of *Law*, and
has Two *Acts* of *Parliament* to defend it. For
tho the Spiritual Privileges of the Priesthood
are independent of the Civil Magistrate, yet
the *Statutes* above-mention'd imply an Assent to
the Charter deliver'd by our Saviour, and
are a fair Acknowledgment of the Power.
And thus, the *Surveyor*, to make a Blow at
the *Clergy*, has charg'd through Gospel and
Law, contradicted the *Bible* and the *Statute-
Book*, and fallen foul upon the Highest Authority both in *Church* and *State.*

But still he *questions, whether the Commission*
of every Christian Priest *be of equal extent
and validity* with that of *the Apostles.* I grant
the first part of his Proposition: That the
Apostles had peculiar Advantages in their
Authority, and that their Jurisdiction was
larger than that of succeeding Priests, or
Bishops either, is not denied. But tho their
Com-

1 Eliz.
14 Car. 2.

Survey. p.348.

Commission was larger, 'twas not more valid than that of the present Priesthood. For this stands upon the Authority of the *New Testament*, upon the Credit of undoubted Succession, and the known Practice of Christendom for almost Seventeen hundred years together. What, tho *they are not call'd immediately by God himself, nor endued with Supernatural and Miraculous Faculties*, does this affect the Credibility of their *Credentials* ? I suppose Princes are the Ministers of God, and deputed to Govern under him; And must the Proof of their Commission depend upon *Miracles* and *immediate* Designation ? Must they be proclaim'd from the Clouds, and Anointed by an Angel from Heaven ? And are not their Subjects to own them till they can make out their Title by Supernatural Evidence; by the Gift of Tongues, and raising the Dead ? The absurdity of these Consequences may inform the *Surveyor*, that there's no need of a Miraculous *Credential* to prove a Delegation from Heaven.

The *Surveyor* in stating the Difference between the Ordinary Priests, and the *Apostles*, makes several Mistakes : And were he in the right, the Dispute is foreign to the Controversy. He affirms the Apostles *Doctrine* had *no other Evidence than their own Affirmation and the Works that they did :* Yes : They had moreover the Completion of Prophecies, and the Agreement of the *Old Testament* ; And these Corroborating Circumstances, were extreamly

Ibid.

Survey, p. 349.

K 2

treamly confiderable. He goes on, and alledges in abatement of the prefent Prieft-
hood, That Perfons of this Order *have no
natural Gifts above other Men, to warrant a*
P. 349, 350. *Pretence to an extraordinary Miffion.* Is the
Bounty of God then confin'd to Privileges
of Nature? Or, Is he not at liberty to chufe
what Officers he pleafes? I conceive the *Surveyor* won't deny this. Had the Apoftles
then any of thefe Advantages above o-
thers? fo far from that, that they feem rather to fall fhort of the common Standard.
Their Apprehenfions at firft were very heavy, and their Reafon check'd by a low Education. And which is more, they were rather chofen for thefe Difadvantages: For this
made their Doctrine the more unqueftion-
able, and the Evidence of their Infpiration
the greater. To fee fuch unpromifing Perfons fo Wife in their Difcourfe, fo Wonderful in their Actions, and fo Unufual in
their Succefs, muft needs convince the World
that God was with them. And thus the *Surveyor's* Affertion is falfe both in Fact, and
Reafoning.

His faying, That this Commiffion of the
Apoftles and their Succeffors, expir'd upon
the Converfion of Princes to Chriftianity,
is a great miftake: The Church is ftill Independent, her Authority unalterable, neither
is fhe in Things purely Spiritual, *fubordinate*
to the Civil Power. This Truth I have elfe-
*Moral Effays,
Office Chap.* where proved at large, and thither I refer the
Reader.
The

The *Surveyor* in speaking to the *Importance* of the Priests *Office*, would not allow him to preside any more in *Gods Worship*, than a *Clerk* in *Parliament* presides over the *House*, because he reads the *Bills*, and *Petitions* to them. It seems then the Relation of the Priest, and the Congregation, is the same with that of the *Clerk to the Parliament*. What would this Author be at? Does he mean, that when the Priest reads the *Bible*, the People may Debate whether it shall pass or not, and divide into *Yeas* and *Noes*, about saying *Amen* to the Lord's Prayer. One would think by his worthy similitude, that the People went to Church to be Worship'd, and that the *Liturgie* was only a Parcel of Humble Petitions put up to the *Parish*. Survey. p.35,2.

The *Surveyor* is extreamly desirous to have a Religious Character expos'd on the *Stage*; But against this Liberty, I have given my Reasons at large; which when the *Surveyor* has replied to, he may possibly hear farther from me. Survey. p.356, Defence, from p. 66, to p.89. View, &c.

My Adversary is now upon arguing against the Plea of *Prescription*, and would gladly make out, that the Heathen *Stage* has Treated the Priests as Coarsly as the Christian. And here *Æschylus* is as surly as before, and won't so much as appear in the Cause. However, *Sophocles* lay in his way, and in he must come; But then this Poet by his Air and Heaviness, looks more like a Prisoner than a Witness; Well! We must hear his Deposi-

tions

tions in his *Ajax Flagellifer*, What then is to be done here? Does the Poet bait a Prieſt like the *Relapſe*? By no means. Does he Repreſent a Prieſt in his *Play*? Not that neither. Then I ſuppoſe he ſpoke ill of him behind his Back? I confeſs that was not as it ſhould be. The beſt on't is, the Miſchief lies in a little compaſs: 'Tis all in a Line or two at the end of the Play: Here the *Chorus*, in regard of the ſurprizing Events they had obſerv'd, are pleas'd to ſay, *That ſeeing, was Believing, and that ne're a Diviner could tell before-hand, how matters would go.*

Ajax. Flag.
'Η πολλὰ βροτοῖς ἔστιν ἰδοῦσιν
Γνῶναι· πρὶν ἰδεῖν δ᾽ ἐδεὶς μάντις
τῶν μελλόντων, ὅ τι πράξει.

Now if this Inſtance muſt have an anſwer, I reply; That Prophets or Diviners held a very ſmall Proportion to the reſt of the Prieſts, ſo that the Cenſure, tho gentle, falls only on the Skirts of the Profeſſion. But then to go even thus far, looks like ſtraining upon *Sophocles*. For the natural meaning of the *Moral* ſeems to be thus; ' That Humane Foreſight is ſhort, and the ' *Future* impenetrable; and therefore People ' ought to Guard accordingly upon the *Pre-* ' *ſent*. But I'm afraid I have been too long upon this Matter, and ſo have uſed the *Reader* a great deal worſe, than *Sophocles* did the *Prophet*.

His

His next Instance in *Jocasta*, is obviated, *Survey.* p. 358.
and answer'd ; and so is that following in *View,* p. 89, 90.
Creon ; who is declar'd by the *Chorus* to be
punish'd for his Haughtiness and Impiety.
However, for once, let's see what the *Sur-*
veyor will make out of *Creon.* Now this
Prince being dissatisfied with *Tiresias's* Discovery in Divination, makes this angry Re-
flection :

Το μαντικὸν ἣ πᾶν φιλάργυρον γένΘ. *Sophoc. Antig.*

That is, *Your Augurs are all a Covetous sort*
of People. Now, tho the Regard which
Creon shew'd *Tiresias* in the preceding Line,
* calls for a soft Construction, yet the *Sur-* * Ου βόλομαι
veyor gives the Text a Mobbish Turn, and ἢ μάντιν ἀ-
foists in some of his own ill Language be- τῆ τῶ χαχῶς.
sides : In his Version it stands thus. *They*
were all a Pack of Mercenary Corrupt Fellows:
This, it seems, is the *English* of φιλαργυρος γένΘ.
At this rate, if he were to Turn St. *Paul's*
Citation from *Aratus,* the Translation of
Τῶ ἢ κ γένΘ ἐσμὲν would run thus : *Act.* 17. 28.
Mankind are a Pack of Fellows of Heavenly
Extraction.

We see what lean Evidence *Sophocles*
proves, tho under the *Surveyor's* Management : I hope I have made him speak a little
fuller on the other side ; * *View,* p. 120.

His first Testimony from *Euripides* is le-
velled only against Soothsaying and Divination,

To

And yet even here he over-tranſlates the Original *, ſpoils the Breeding of the Character, and makes Generals rail like Carmen.

* *A vain-glorious raſcally Race, Surv.* p. 359.

And in the ſame *Play* he Tranſlates ἀνὴρ *Fellow*, and makes the beſt Word in the *Greek*, the worſt in the *Engliſh*. Farther, we may take notice, that theſe warm Expreſſions were ſpoken againſt *Calchas* the Augur: And tho' one of them was deliver'd by *Achilles*, who was all Paſſion and Violence, yet 'twas in the abſence of the Perſon Cenſur'd. And as for *Calchas*, his Intereſt is great, and his Figure creditable in the *Play* *.

—iracundus, inexorabilis acer, jura negat ſibi nata, nihil nonarroget armis. Horat. de Art. Poet.
* *Eurip. Iphig. in Aulid.* p. 44. & alib.
View, p. 120, 121.

His Inſtance in *Pentheus*, and likewiſe what he offers from *Seneca*, is anſwer'd in the *View*, where the *Reader* may ſee an over-ballance of Evidence for the other ſide.

But we muſt leave the Prieſts, and go on to the Gods their Maſters: Now theſe the *Surveyor* pretends were uſed with great Freedom by the *Antients*.

Survey, p. 360.

He begins with *Sophocles*, and objects the Rants of *Ajax*, *Creon*, and *Philoctetes*; but here his Charge is ſomewhat inhumane. Theſe Characters have ſmarted ſeverely for their Impiety: Now Perſons that have ſuffer'd the Law, ſhould not be reproach'd with their Crimes: And therefore in *Scotland*

View, p. 88, 89, 93.

land they fay when a Man is Hanged, he's
Juſtified. But the *Surveyor* wants time for a
Collection out of this Poet : Not unlikely :
People that have nothing to pay, are gene- Surv. p. 360, 361.
rally in Haſte.

    Euripides is once more ſummon'd : Now View, p. 94
this Poet, I granted, had ſome Profane Paſſages uncorrected : And 'tis well my Conceſ-
ſion was thus frank, for I perceive the *Surveyor* can hardly prove it : However his Performance muſt be Examin'd.

His firſt Citation from the *Hecuba* is the
beſt. But here he loſes more in his Skill,
than he gains in his Luck. For he quite mi-
ſtakes the meaning of part of *Talthybius's*
Expoſtulation;

$$\text{Ω, Ζεῦ, τί λέξω ; πότερά σ' ἀνθρώπους ὁρᾶν ;}$$ Hec. p. 17.
$$\text{Ἢ δόξαν ἄλλως τίω ὃ κεκτῆσθαι μάτην ;}$$

    Which he thus Tranſlates. *O Jupiter !
What ſhall I ſay ? ſhould Mankind addreſs* Surv. p. 361.
themſelves to you ? &c. Whereas it ſhould
have been rendred thus. *O Jupiter ! I'm at
a ſtand whether Humane Affairs are part of your
Adminiſtration, or not,* &c. But I ſhall purſue the Advantage no farther. This might
be a Piece of Honeſt Ignorance for ought I
know : And no Man can Play more then he
ſees. But then he ſhould be a little cautious
not to venture out of his depth, till he can
Swim better.

Polym-

Polymneſtor in this Tragedy is another In-
ſtance how far the *Surveyor* is to be truſted.
The Words muſt be tranſcrib'd ; in which
this Prince Complains of the uncertainty of
Proſperity , and the ſuddain Turns of
Fate ;

Θεῦ ὐκ ἔςιν ὐδὲν πιςὸν, ὀυτ ἐυδοξία,
Ὀυτ' ἀῦ καλῶς πράσσοντα, μὴ πράξειν κακῶς.
Φύρεσι δ' ἀῦϑ' οἱ θεοὶ πάλιντε ἡ πρόσω,
ταραγμὸν ἐντιθέντες, ὡς ἀγνωσία
Σέβωμεν ὰυτές.

Let's now ſee what *Engliſh* the *Surveyor*
Survey. p.361,can afford us to this *Greek.* *Oh, what a ſlip-*
pery thing is Humane Grandeur, which is never
ſecure ? Thus far all's well. But then the
Remainder is wretchedly wreſted into A-
theiſm and Miſconſtruction : —— *The Gods*
(ſays he) *perplex and harraſs Mankind, that*
our Ignorance may ſupport their Altars, and Wor-
ſhip. But the Poet's meaning ſtands thus.
The Gods make Humane Affairs floating, and un-
certain ; that ſo our Ignorance of Future Events,
may prevent the fancy of Independence, and make
us apply to Heaven for a better Protection. Now
this is a Sence of Piety, inſtead of Prophaneneſs. And to juſtifie the *Tranſlation,* I appeal not only to the *Text,* and *Latin* Verſion, but to the *Greek Scholiaſt,* who is ex-
preſsly for it. Farther : If there had been
any thing of Prophaneneſs in this Reflecti-
on, *Polymneſtor* paid dearly for't. For ſoon
after

after his Eyes are pluck'd out, and his Children murther'd before him *.

To proceed. *Electra*'s Expostulation is horribly misrepresented. This Lady seeing *Helena* upon her return from *Troy*, and that she brought back her Beauty with her Infamy, makes this Remark upon't.

* *Eurip. Hec.* p. 36, 40.

> Ὦ φύσις ἐν ἀνθρώποισιν ὡς μέγ' εἶ κακὸν,
> Σωτήριόν τε τοῖς καλῶς κεκτημένοις.

Eurip. Orist. p. 51.

That is, *Advantages of Person are a misfortune to some People; But extreamly serviceable to such as make a right use of them.* Here the *Surveyor* bestirs him notably. He keeps the last Line to himself, maims the Period, and then rigs out this Pious Translation;

O Nature, what a Curse art thou upon Mortals! As much as to say, He has found a Heathen President for the Blasphemy of the *Moderns:* Whereas 'tis notoriously evident, that here is not the least glance against Providence; And that only the Endowments and Advantages of Nature are meant by the Expression.

Surv. 362.

Orestes is no more the *Surveyor*'s Friend than *Electra* his Sister. For when *Menelaus* question'd him about the Murther of his Mother, he pleads the *Oracle* in his Excuse. And when the other was surpriz'd at the singularity of the Order, He replies,

> Δουλεύομεν θεοῖς ὅτι ποτ' εἰσὶ θεοί.

Orest. p. 5

That

That is, 'We are not to difpute the Gods
'Commands, but obey them, for the Di-
'vine Nature is too big for Humane Under-
'ftandings. And if the *Surveyor* thinks this
too much a Paraphrafe, *Oreftes* fhall fpeak in
his own Tranflation. 'Tis thus : *We ferve
the Gods whatever they be.* Why then, it
feems, he did not queftion their Being, but
thought Religion very well worth the minding. Yes : His Piety appears farther in his
next anfwer, for when *Menelaus* feem'd to
wonder why *Apollo* did not refcue him from
his Misfortune ; He tells him,

Survey. p. 362.

Μέλλει, τὸ θεῖον δ' ἐςὶ τοιῦτον φύσιν.

That is, as the *Scholiaft* interprets, The
'Gods are not fuddain in their Adminiftra-
'tions ; But take time in Rewards, and Pu-
'nifhments, to Try the Good, and Recove
'the Evil.

His Objection from the *Cyclops* is fully
prevented in the *View*. However the Poet
muft be cited, and the Gyant brought in
for the fake of the Civil Tranflation. Befides, a little *Greek*, tho nothing to the purpofe, has a Face of Learning, and looks Big
upon the *Englifh Reader*.

View, p. 94.

Survey, p. 362.

In the *Jon*, by Tranflating κακὸς *Rafcal*
and ιυνάτως Whoremafter, he makes *Creufa*
and her Servant much coarfer than they are
in *Euripides*. 'Tis true the Servant being
moved with the fuppos'd ill Ufage of his
Miftrefs

Jon. p. 333, 334.

Miftrefs, propos'd the firing of *Apollo*'s
Temple ; but immediately he recollects himfelf, and advifes her to another Revenge,
more in her Power.

To conclude with *Euripides*, *Hecuba*, fays
the *Surveyor*, thinks the Gods καxὺς συμμάχυς,
bad Friends ; He fhould have faid *fluggifh*,
and then he had been right. As for *Seneca*
he ftands barr'd : Why then is his Athei-
ftical *Chorus* produced, and why in the Verfion of the Earl of *Rochefter* ? Was this
Tranfition made for the Benefit of the Publick, or in Honour of the Deceas'd ? Not
the latter, for that Noble Lord, abhor'd fuch
Prophane Liberties at his Death. Thus, to
Refrefh the Blemifhes of his Life, is the
greateft Outrage to his Memory : 'Tis almoft
enough to raife him upon the *Surveyor*, to
make his Ghoft refent the Ufage, and flafh Correction in his Face ; But after all, 'tis highly
improbable that the *Chorus* fpoke the *Poet's
Opinion*, if, as *Heinfius*, *Scaliger*, and others
believe, 'twas written by *Seneca* the Philofopher : For every Body knows he was far
enough from being an Atheift.

And now we have done with Authorities ;
And here, tho the *Surveyor* has but very bad
Luck with his *Poets*, yet he has taken great
care to conceal the Misfortune ; For in his
Citations he mentions neither *Act*, nor *Page*,
but refers to the *Plays* at large. This, I confefs, is the right way to difcourage the
Reader's Enquiry, and make him rather Believe, than go Look. And

Jon. p. 335.

Survey. p. 362.

Troad. 118.

See *View*, p. 94.

Surv. p. 363.

And now I may safely affirm, That several single *Plays* of the *Moderns*, * have not only more, but some bolder Passages of Prophaneness, than all he has cited from the *Antients* put together. And which is harder still, I have made but a slender Discovery of the *English Stage*. Thus some People Refine upon Heathenism ; Thus they improve upon their Creed, and make amends in their Lives, for the odds of their Understanding !

* See *View*, and *Defence*, *Pref*.

Survey. p. 367.

In the Close of all, the *Surveyor offers Hypothetically*, as he calls it, that is faintly, to justifie the *Stage-Freedoms* with the *Nobility*. But, by his favour, this Ridiculous Character must either be drawn for single Persons, or Quality in general : Now either way his Satyr falls under his own Lash ; For from hence it must follow, that he who makes a *Lord* of a *Fool, makes a Fool of a Lord*, which he grants is *no Compliment*. But the *Surveyor* having not reply'd to my Reasons against this Liberty, I need say nothing more upon the Argument.

Survey. p. 365.

View, p. 175. *Defence*. p. 25. to p. 31.

I have now done with the *Surveyor*; and heartily wish him a better Subject : For a bad Cause, besides its own Evil, is apt to produce a resembling Defence: It often runs an Author upon Calumny, Coarse Expedients, and Little Management : Which, as they are no sure Methods to raise a Character ; so, at one time or other, they'l certainly displease a Man's self.

THE END.